The Mysterion

THE
MYSTERION

Rumi and the Secret of Becoming Fully Human

KABIR HELMINSKI

SHAMBHALA

Shambhala Publications, Inc.
2129 13th Street
Boulder, Colorado 80302
www.shambhala.com

© 2023 by Kabir Helminski

Cover art: iStock.com / Gunay Aliyeva
Cover design: Lauren Michelle Smith
Interior design: Lora Zorian

9 8 7 6 5 4 3 2 1

First Edition
Printed in the United States of America

Shambhala Publications makes every effort
to print on acid-free, recycled paper.
Shambhala Publications is distributed worldwide
by Penguin Random House, Inc., and its subsidiaries.

Library of Congress Cataloging-in-Publication Data
Names: Helminski, Kabir Edmund, 1947– author.
Title: The mysterion: Rumi and the secret of becoming fully human /
Kabir Helminski.
Description: Boulder, Colorado : Shambhala, [2023] |
Includes bibliographical references.
Identifiers: LCCN 2022026416 | ISBN 9781645471448 (trade paperback)
Subjects: LCSH: Spirituality—Islam. | Sufism. |
Jalāl al-Dīn Rūmī, Maulana, 1207–1273.
Classification: LCC BP189.6 .H45 2023 |
DDC 297.4—dc23/eng/20220723
LC record available at https://lccn.loc.gov/2022026416

Contents

CONTENTS

PREFACE

Rumi and Humanness

DEAR READER, you have a right to know what you are getting into with this book. This is not an analysis of Rumi as a literary or historical phenomenon. This book is written by someone who has practiced the applied spirituality of Sufism for more than fifty years, adapting it to the mentality and culture of the present era.

The themes in this book are focused around the soul in its relationship to the Divine. "The Mysterion" represents the intersection of the soul with the Divine. This is just one possible approach to the vast corpus of Rumi.

This book is assembled from teachings shared at various retreats and gatherings. This author is thankful for the privilege of being called to serve a community of sincere spiritual seekers without whom this book would not exist. It is in the interaction of the expressed needs of people at a particular time that this work emerged. It is also an attempt to convey traditional knowledge in a contemporary way. Sufism is a living tradition that is continually creative and yet in alignment with a fundamental Reality.

Rumi is timeless because his primary subject is the soul's relationship with the Divine. His genius is that he uses every aspect of our lives to reveal the beauty, generosity, and purposefulness of existence. His writings show the interconnected nature of the human and spiritual realms. He describes his six-volume masterpiece, the *Mathnawi*, as "the workshop of Oneness." Through his words we perceive and confirm that there is a mutual attraction between the soul and its Source.

The interrelationship of self, heart, soul, and Spirit is the beginning of understanding our place in this universe. For Rumi, human selfhood is the key to a vast and beautiful mystery. With this knowledge we can better practice the art of being human.

If you have heard the sometimes tender, sometimes soaring improvisations of the Mevlevi ney, you have a sense of the spiritual qualities of Rumi's tradition. Or if you have unexpectedly found in a few lines from Rumi the expression of a truth you have always known but never heard spoken, welcome.

It is the Mysterion by which the Divine is experienced in the depths of the soul. While the contemporary world sometimes seems to be in danger of spinning off into a technocratic post-human dystopia, we urgently need to experience the intrinsic meaning of being human. If we human beings can learn to connect to the Infinite, where it is closest to us, in ourselves, we may fulfill our purpose in being human.

A Note on Language and Translation

THIS IS MEANT TO BE A BOOK OF KNOWLEDGE. Writing about "spirituality" is full of hazards and challenges—of presuming to know more than we in fact can know, of overintellectualizing, of the limitations of language, and of the misunderstandings that arise from the meanings we associate with certain words like *God*, *sin*, or *consciousness*. And yet there is no knowledge more important than the knowledge of the true possibilities of our existence.

Writing in the English language also has its particular challenges. English is a very rich language, drawing from so many linguistic streams—Anglo-Saxon, Germanic, Latin, and more recently from all the languages of the world. But it has never been a language of revelation. Sanskrit, Hebrew, Arabic, Persian, even Greek to some extent, are languages with profound spiritual vocabularies in which key words acquire a durability and depth of meaning through the various contexts in which those words appear. In English, we are forced to forge a spiritual vocabulary by creating a spiritual glossary, by defining what we mean when we say *soul*, or *spirit*, or *consciousness*. The glossary at the end of this book is an essential part of the book.

Sufism has a deep and comprehensive spiritual vocabulary, drawn primarily from Qur'anic Arabic, a vocabulary shared by the various languages that have been enculturated by Islam: Persian, Turkish, Urdu, in addition to Arabic. It is an indication of the power of the Qur'anic vocabulary that so many of its terms have resisted translation and been adopted into other languages. The same process is even now happening in the English language as a literature of Sufism and Islam is being created.

Translations of Rumi, other Sufi texts, the hadiths,[1] and the Qur'an are the result of decades of work as a translator and writer. Unless otherwise noted, all the translations in this book are my own or done in collaboration with my wife Camille. The selections in this book are sometimes close to the foundational translations of the Islamic scholar Reynold A. Nicholson (for Rumi) and Muhammad Asad, the great twentieth-century Qur'anic translator and commentator. I hope that I have been judicious in what I have introduced of my own understanding and sense of literary style.

In the vocabulary of Sufism, certain words are not mere labels to name "things" but lenses through which to "see."

Language is a divine gift that helps us to discern the levels of reality and ultimately to guide us to a realm beyond words. We cannot overestimate the value of clarifying the vocabulary of the spiritual path, for through that vocabulary we glimpse a reality beyond words.

The Mysterion

1

Story of the Honest Man Meeting Khidr

AN HONEST AND SUCCESSFUL MAN who had attained many of the satisfactions of ordinary existence nevertheless felt that his life was somehow incomplete. He had read a wide range of books about spirituality, and even journeyed to foreign lands to experience different spiritual cultures. Over the course of his life he had practiced two or three spiritual traditions for various periods of time, experiencing some beneficial states but always returning to his ordinary state of dissatisfaction and incompleteness. There must have been some benefit in all this searching and spiritual work, but he honestly could not assess where he was on the spiritual path, and his hunger for truth would not let him rest. At long last he had traveled to the shrine of one of the great Sufis of the past. After prayers and meditation in the sanctuary of the Pir, he had gone to the *Hamushan*, the place of the "silent ones," and was sitting among the graves of generations of those who had served that great saint.

It was there that he encountered a nondescript man dressed in dark green who approached him in a friendly manner. He had with him a container of hot Turkish tea that he kindly shared as he began the following conversation.

"You are a seeker of truth, and you have not been able to content yourself with the common superficial satisfactions of life, and you suspect there is more for you to understand. Close your eyes and allow me to reveal some indications about the path to truth."

You may have begun to suspect that the man in green was the

legendary and immortal Khidr. Now, in the mind's eye of the honest man, a scenario began to unfold in which he saw some people whose faces seemed dark, whose tone of voice was shrill, and he wondered who these people were.

"We are those who attached ourselves to self-promoting teachers who promised us secret knowledge and attracted followers with their cultish mystique. We competed for attention among ourselves, and we substituted a shallow idea of self-development in place of true service."

Next, he saw a tall apartment building that seemed to be constructed with the pages of books, pages that had, however, turned into drywall and concrete. The furnishings of each condo were made from letters and words, and the residents were continually busy rearranging the syntax and vocabulary of their habitations. "We thought that our intelligence was the supreme virtue, and we conflated book knowledge with spiritual experience. We still keep busy trying to arrange the words into a meaningful conclusion that will free us."

"But did that bookishness alone condemn you to this situation?"

"We were the smartest of the smart; we clung to our sense of superiority and had no patience for those with simpler minds than ours."

Finally he was taken to a place where he saw people reclining at ease, with smiles frozen upon their faces. They seemed to be talking to themselves as if in a daydream, and he asked these people who they were. As if in a chorus, he heard their voices speak within himself: "We are those who followed our own inclinations, mistaking our own whims and desires for the will of God, and preferring pleasure and ease to the signs of truth along the way."

"But at least you don't seem so unhappy."

"Because we chose our own immediate satisfactions above all else and called this happiness."

"Was it not real happiness?"

"Happiness is no substitute for truth if happiness imprisons you."

Just then the visions ended and he found himself sitting in the graveyard again with the green man at his side.

"Perhaps you're coming to see your journey up to this point with new eyes? This is what realization feels like. You're beginning to see how much of your life has been wasted seeking personal gratification, going from one path to another, avoiding the truth more often than committing to it."

"And yet here in the graveyard of the great saint, I met the one legendary and immortal being who few people ever meet."

"Yes, and only because at a certain point in your life you were sincere enough to make an honest prayer, a call from deep in the mystery of yourself, and now your call is being answered."

The honest man now felt an overwhelming sense of remorse and the desire to seek only the truth, but just then Khidr stood up and, speaking softly, began to walk away. "You can't follow me now because I must go back to the ordinary world, the world of half-truths and confused people. The place where I have to do my work."

And as the green man walked away, the honest man felt forsaken and bereft. But as he looked around himself in the graveyard of dervishes, everything around him *was the same and yet not the same*. The gravestones tilted by the hands of time, the rosebushes budding and flowering, the clouds sailing against a cobalt-blue sky, and he was standing in the Land of Reality.

2

From Ego to Soul

P EOPLE STRIVE IN SO MANY WAYS for so many things in this world; a few strive for a spiritual discipline that leads to a direct experience of reality. The "Land of Reality" is not other than the world we live in, but it takes the awakening of spiritual perception to see it and know it. The sacred interpenetrates existence and yet mysteriously goes unperceived. A life that does not lead to an increasing awareness of the sacred is a life without reality—shallow and superficial. There are potentially many paths that lead, ultimately, to a perception of the beauty and love inherent in the universe.

Some rare human beings have penetrated so deeply into the nature of reality that they have been thoroughly transformed by the experience. By their very presence they have had a transformative effect on others. Rumi is one of those rare human beings, and the legacy of knowledge he has left for humanity is incomparable. From one perspective he is the culmination of six centuries of Islamic spiritual civilization. From another perspective he is an example of what humanity has yet to achieve.

The traditional word for Sufism, *tasawwuf*, means "the process of purification." That is why in Sufism it is not recommended to start a campaign, put on a uniform, or raise a banner, but rather polish the mirror of your heart, be thankful in every circumstance, be aware with every breath.

In every society and culture, human beings are culturally conditioned by prejudices and assumptions that impede their ability to fully appreciate each other's humanity and the possibilities of human existence.

At its best, Sufism is a framework for transformation that can help us to purify our perception and remove the distorting factors in ourselves. Only then can we experience, be aware of, and perceive the mercy, generosity, and beauty of reality.

The Self-Evident Value of True Spirituality

Egoism is a false coin that no one really would want to buy or sell with if they could see it clearly. Those who trade in it end up disillusioned in the end. A healthy humility is innately more pleasing and attractive than conceit. A selfless love is infinitely more beautiful than self-serving privilege. Compassionate cooperation builds a prosperous community; cutthroat competition undermines human relationships. True spirituality is self-evident and proves its value even in this mundane world.

For those who sincerely want to distinguish what is truly real and of lasting value, there are spiritual laws to be discovered and verified. Meanwhile, the world established through false, egoistic values cannot satisfy the human heart.

Despite the relentless propagandizing of commercial and political forces, the heart continues to seek something real. Despite the attempt to commodify every aspect of our lives, the soul rightfully rebels and seeks to break the spell of mass suggestibility.

So many forces in today's world routinely use emotional conditioning and social engineering for the purpose of control. Most people are very suggestible and are easily subjected to emotional and mental manipulation. It is only necessary to provide a powerful emotional experience in some form of mass suggestion to convince people that something is "true." Pharaohs and emperors, clergy and gurus have used pomp and ceremonies, symbols and monuments to convince people of their power and authority.

Emotional and mental conditioning should not be confused

with spiritual development. Being emotionally committed and mentally convinced has little to do with purifying our perception. Wearing pink-tinted sunglasses will change how you see things but it will not improve your vision, especially if you are half-blind.

The effects of mass suggestibility need to be removed through a gradual process of self-observation and reeducation. But there are other, subtler veils that must also be lifted. The outer pharaoh is easier to unseat than the inner pharaoh (or inner Cleopatra). Political propaganda is easier to discard than the lies we tell ourselves. We must confront all sorts of personal defenses and illusions: our vanity, judgments, self-importance, and fears.

Whether or not we believe in an eternal soul, or higher worlds, or heavenly realms, there is a practical, empirical work that can expand our sense of reality and open us to dimensions of experience that can rightfully be considered spiritual. This work is not undertaken for the sake of "earning heaven" but for the sake of self-knowledge and discovering who we truly are. In time, we realize that what is most precious and real is invisible, that the true life is the life of the soul, and the true work is the work of the soul. What much of humanity is unknowingly searching for is a relationship with a spiritual dimension that can heal our estranged souls and satisfy our restless hearts.

Rumi offers this analogy:

When a man goes to the bathhouse, he gets warm. Everywhere he goes in the bathhouse the fire is with him; although he is warmed by the effect of the fire's heat, he cannot see it. When he comes out and actually sees the fire, he realizes that he was warmed by the fire, that the heat of the bathhouse was from the fire. Man's being is a marvelous "bathhouse." In him is the "heat" of the mind, the spirit, and the soul. Only when you come out of this bathhouse and go to the other world will you actually see the essence of the mind. You will witness the essence of the soul and the essence of the spirit.

You will realize that your cleverness was due to the "heat" of the mind, that temptations and deceits were due to the lower self, and that your vitality was due to the spirit. You will see plainly the essence of each one.

So long as you remain inside the "bathhouse," however, you cannot see the "fire" sensibly, only through its effect. It would be like taking someone who has never seen running water and throwing him blindfolded into water. He feels something wet and soft against his body, but he doesn't know what it is. When the blindfold is taken off, he realizes that it is water. Before, he knew it through its effect, but now he sees its essence.

Therefore, beg of God and make your request of Him that it not be all in vain. God says, "Call upon Me, and I will hear you" [40:60].

Signs of the Unseen [Fihi ma fihi], Discourse 45

The Mysterion: The Secret of Our Humanness

An acorn is an oak tree in embryonic form. It would be foolish for an acorn to think that its growth potential, what it is destined to become, is its own doing. In the design of the universe there are such potentials to be fulfilled. Nothing is without purpose, but in the case of the human being, the fulfillment of that purpose is not inevitable; it is a matter of conscious choice. We are born as incomplete beings; our completion is dependent on our own free will actualizing the potential within us. This is something unique to the human being. Other creatures follow their own natures, but the human being has been given the gift, and the curse, of free will.

"There is no power nor strength but with the Divine" is an often recited prayer among Muslims, whose efficacy and value is mentioned in numerous hadiths. The great mystics, who were the most highly developed of human beings, have verified this truth. They glimpsed in the moments of highest attainment that everything was owed to the Divine Reality. Their great discipline, practice, and love—their personal sovereignty—grew out of their own relationship to that greater Reality. They demonstrated that the sovereign individual is the conscious actualizer of that Divine Agency; individuality is the instrument through which Divine Will is made manifest. If this is puzzling, confusing, or difficult to grasp, read on. Maybe Rumi can make it clearer:

"In the city of your dreams you found nothing lacking except a noble person."[1] In a city where you find all the beauties, pleasures, delights, and various adornments of nature, yet you didn't find one intelligent person, it would have been better the other way around! That city is the human being. If it has a hundred thousand accomplishments but not its intrinsic meaning, it would be better for it to be in ruins. If it does have that intrinsic meaning, it doesn't matter that it has no outward embellishments. The Mysterion must be there for it to flourish. In whatever state a human being may be, may that Mysterion be concerned with God, and may any external preoccupations in no way hinder that inner concern. In whatever state a pregnant woman may be—war or peace, eating or sleeping—the baby is growing, is being strengthened, and is receiving sensations in her womb without her being aware of it. Mankind likewise is "pregnant" with that Mysterion. "But the human being undertook it (the responsibility offered by God): truly the human was unjust to himself, and foolish" [*Surah al-Ahzab* 33:72], but God does not leave one in that injustice and foolishness. If out of a human being's apparent burden come companionship, sympathy, and a thousand acquaintances, then consider what marvelous friendships and acquaintances will issue out of the Mysterion to which a human being gives birth after death. The Mysterion is necessary in order for a human being to flourish. It is like the root of a tree: although it is hidden from view, its effects are apparent on the branches. Even if one or two branches break off, when the root is strong, the tree will continue to grow. If, however, the root suffers damage, neither branch nor leaf will survive.

Signs of the Unseen[2] *[Fihi ma fihi]*, Discourse 50

What Rumi is calling "the Mysterion" is the point of contact with the Infinite in our souls. As obscure or esoteric as this may sound, it can be conceived and understood through a very simple proposal: all our human capacities and virtues are sourced in a higher-order reality and are manifested in existence either spontaneously or through an act of will. The individual human being, even the sovereign individual, is not the creator of consciousness, will, intelligence, or love but the reflector of these qualities and capacities. Like a mirror, we can reflect a spectrum of qualities depending on how polished and clean our mirror is. Likewise, our mirrors can become distorted and corroded by egoism and negativity. So there is practical work to be done removing distortions from our souls, and on a positive note, aligning ourselves with this higher-order reality through humility, reverence, surrender, and love.

> You, ignorant of the marrow, deceived by the skin,
> be aware. The Beloved is at the center of your soul.
> The essence of the body is sensation
> and the essence of the senses is the soul.
> When you transcend body, senses, and soul,
> all is Hu. There is only Hu.[3]
>
> Quatrain 322

3

What Do We Mean by the Soul?

I F SOMEBODY WERE TO ASK YOU about your soul, what picture comes to mind? What do you think of? Some ethereal substance lodged in your chest? Some subtle specter associated with yourself? A part of you that, although rarely considered, is eternal and may or may not be prepared for heaven or whatever comes after this life? Is the soul a thing? Or is it yourself—your true identity?

Before we can attempt to answer these questions, we would do well to look at our own experience. Much of the time, what we take to be ourselves is our thinking. We not only think but we think about ourselves, which sometimes leads to quite a muddle. We each have an idea of who we are, and we think within the framework of this idea of ourselves. We also have characteristic behaviors and personality features that we take to be ourselves, as well as a body that is our everyday reference point.

But when we speak of the soul, we mean something more essential than this body—an identity, a consciousness. If we have looked deeply within ourselves, practiced sufficient meditation, or come near enough to death, we may have experienced some of what we are beyond our body. We may, for instance, have experienced ourselves as simple, unqualified presence—a state more fundamental than our thoughts, emotions, and behaviors. This is a subtler aspect of ourselves.

Whether we believe the soul is destined for eternal life beyond the body, we can at least agree that each of us has an inner being, the condition of which has something to do with our quality of life. It may be that we give more attention to the outer needs of life than the needs of our inner being. Perhaps we have made the mistake of thinking that the state of our inner being depends more than anything else on our outer material conditions. Yet it is through nonmaterial qualities of experience and feelings such as conscience, contentment, wonder, love, and yearning that this inner being makes itself known to us.

> O head, you are cause within cause within cause.
> O body, you are wonder within wonder within wonder.
> O heart, you are searching within searching within searching.
> O soul, you are joy within joy within joy.
>
> Quatrain 1668

Forming a Soul

Within the context of Sufi metaphysics, "soul" can be understood as the result of the union of self and Spirit. Spirit is our innermost consciousness (Holy Spirit; *Ruh*, in Arabic). It is that which is beyond material existence and yet accessible to us through our inmost consciousness. As in the analogy of the fire that warms the bathhouse, that "fire" that produces the mind is this Spirit. You would see the essence of the mind, the essence of the soul, and the essence of the Spirit if you could come out of the bathhouse.

The self without the presence of Spirit is merely ego, a counterfeit self, which is governed by self-centered thoughts and emotions.

This union of self and Spirit is not like the addition of two elements that immediately produces a definite outcome, like 1+9=10. It's more like a process; something like the sun ripening a fruit. This union of self and Spirit is something that gradually matures, and when the fruit, the soul, is matured, this soul acquires substance and structure. That is why it is said in some teachings that we do not automatically have a soul but that we must acquire one through a spiritual process, through our spiritual work.

What are the signs that someone is lacking soul? To be dominated by the random attractions of the world, bouncing between likes and dislikes, shifting from one subpersonality to another, from one intention to another, changing one's mind constantly, living without a center—this is the state of the ego-self without the benefit of Spirit.

This false, counterfeit self has little constancy because it is more of an effect than a cause, more of a reaction to circumstances and conditions than an agent with independent will and being.

What are the signs that someone has begun to acquire a soul? Such a person will prove to have more constancy of being. Qualities such as presence, intentionality, and kindness will be evident in their everyday life.

Eventually, as the soul develops, it will show this constancy even in dreams. The self under the influence of Spirit becomes receptive to positive influences even to the depths of the subconscious mind. What flows forth from Spirit is the ultimate intelligence and virtue.

The more the self is imbued with Spirit, the more the soul can be said to be durable, able to sustain awareness and intention. On the other hand, the self that has only an intermittent, weak relationship with Spirit will be more forgetful and easily distracted.

That's why, especially in the beginning, it is so important to be intentional in relation to one's spiritual commitments.

> On Resurrection Day God will ask,
> "During this reprieve I gave you,
> what have you produced for Me?
> Through what work have you reached your life's end?
> For what end have your food
> and your strength been consumed?
> Where have you dimmed the luster of your eye?
> Where have you dissipated your five senses?
> You have spent your seeing, hearing, intelligence,
> and the pure celestial substances;
> what have you purchased from the earth?
> I gave you hands and feet as tools
> for tilling the soil of good works;
> when did they gain a will of their own?"

Mathnawi III, 2149–53

Himma, *the Meta-Intention of Spiritual Resolve*

The spiritual teacher is very familiar with the ploys of the false self, how it interferes with peoples' spiritual intentions, distracting and subverting them. Yet without giving priority to such intentions, there is little chance of transforming the false self and developing the soul.

The remedy for the insincerity of the scattered self is *himma*, the spiritual resolve to focus all of one's faculties and efforts toward attaining intimacy with Allah, the union of self and Spirit.

The work of the soul must be given the highest priority, but it need not displace or interfere with one's everyday responsibilities.

This is because the intention to awaken happens on a metalevel, just as presence is a meta-awareness on a higher level than physical sensations, emotions, and thoughts. It is an intention to hold the contents of the psyche in an expanded field of awareness, which gives an entirely new perspective. From this vantage point, above the relentless clash of opposites, above the many decisions and intentions of mechanical life, it is possible to hold a higher intention.

One example of how this meta-intention is described in Islam is the concept of "the Covenant" (*al-Mithaq*). All souls that would ever exist were gathered in pre-eternity, and Allah asked them, "Am I not your Sustainer (*Rabb*)?" To which certain souls replied, "*Bala!*" (Yes!). Remembering the Covenant with Allah is one form of that meta-intention that accompanies *himma*, spiritual resolve. Incidentally, those souls who answered yes in pre-eternity, when they meet in the course of this earthly life, recognize each other and feel as if they have always known each other.

With this kind of meta-intention, we practice fully accepting and attending to the responsibilities of our lives, simultaneously aware that we belong to Allah, avoiding the traps the *nafs* (ego) might otherwise fall into. In time, this meta-awareness becomes our natural way of life.

———

Having described the interrelationship of ego, soul, and Spirit, we can now consider the effects of the domination of ego at the level of societies and the world. Then, after recognizing our true situation, we can explore the possibilities for healing our estrangement from Reality and for attaining our spiritual potential as truly human beings.

4

Humanity in Confrontation with Itself

H AVING EXPLORED in the previous chapter the nature of the soul and our individual relationship with the Divine, we now take a closer look at ourselves. We cannot sincerely approach spiritual practice unless we know what we are dealing with.

What would it be like to see our inner selves reflected in a mirror? Would we be willing to face ourselves in such a mirror? The pages that follow will attempt to hold a mirror to the typical human self. I ask your forbearance. This will not be the most enjoyable chapter of this book, but it's where we must begin.

A mirror does not judge or blame. It only reflects what is there. It cannot be bribed or coerced into doing anything but reflecting what is there. You have the mirror, though you may not know it. I hope this book will help you discover your own mirror and how to keep it polished and clear.

Lurking in the shadows of almost all human difficulties and problems is a psychic usurper, a counterfeit self, that controls our thoughts, feelings, and behaviors. It is essentially a defensive, reactive, self-serving mechanism within the psyche.

In a relatively healthy, integrated individual, its influence may be minimal, only occasionally triggered by extreme circumstances when we feel our security or self-worth threatened. In most human beings, it remains just outside conscious awareness, manipulating our overt actions, coloring our thoughts and perceptions.

In certain cases, it can play a dominant role, establishing its tyranny over the subtler and kinder functions of the heart and mind, and eventually exercising that tyranny in its relationships with others and within its own environment.

The issue of the dominance of the false self is not an idle question because, while pretending to be our protector, it is actually our worst enemy.

This counterfeit self takes itself very seriously and tends toward extreme self-righteousness. It builds a shell around itself that shields it from the rest of the mind and heart.

It has very little awareness of its own complex motivations. Being in a defensive mode most of the time, it is unaware of its own darkness and negative impulses, and it tends to project its image of evil out onto the world. The enemy is entirely out there to be confronted, while the evil within not only escapes confrontation but is denied altogether in the name of its own righteous cause.

And just as the false self in a pathological condition can tyrannize the whole of one's psyche, so too can collective expressions of the false self—a collective of pathological egos—empower criminal behavior, authoritarianism, fascism, and all forms of tyranny.

Today humanity is in a state of confrontation with itself, between that side of ourselves that can see and that can be an objective witness, that can look itself in the mirror; in contrast to that part of ourselves that proffers lies and is mired in self-delusion. In other words, there is a struggle between those parts of ourselves that "know" and those parts of ourselves that "don't know."

The part of us that "knows" represents a dimension of ourselves informed by the heart and by higher consciousness. It is a state of mind that is spacious and motivated by love. It can gain some perspective on the false self and moderate its demands. It can laugh and let go. The part of us that "doesn't know" is reactive, controlling, self-righteous, and motivated by fear. The false self will take extreme measures to protect and defend itself. What it is trying to defend is, however, an obstinate yet fragile illusion, so its defenses are ultimately doomed to failure, but not before wreaking havoc within the psyche and in the world.

The Culture of Hyper-Individualism

How often have we seen ourselves and others, despite the good that we intend, falling victim to the blind drives of our desires and opinions? How often have we seen the unity of purpose undermined by focusing on our differences rather than what we have in common? And how often in today's world do we find it difficult to be unified and harmonized with others, whether through custom, ritual, worship, or everyday social interaction?

Personal choice and individual opinion have become enshrined as the secular religion of modern civilization. We have made following our own whims and desires the default center of our lives. We drive alone in our own cars, order our own meals, entertain ourselves in private. The power of all of our technology has been employed to make it easier to follow our individualistic impulses.

We have even been spared the inconvenience of our interactions with each other. So much of our communications are suspended in an electronic simulation of our real presence. Messages, apologies, excuses, proposals, mediated by technology, float in digital reservoirs of meaning, await our attention, and can be stored or deleted with a fingertip. In almost every area of our lives we are faced with a bewildering array of personal but often meaningless choices. This is the kind of world we find ourselves in.

All human beings seem to be restlessly, compulsively seeking to relieve some anxiety. Most search for this relief in pleasure, romance, money, social recognition, or personal power. Some seek relief in friendship, community, or love. A few seek relief in knowledge or artistic expression.

All too often these different goals contradict or undermine each other. The desire for power undermines community, romance competes with love, money issues disrupt friendships, the need for pleasure battles with the longing for knowledge. Our lives become complex equations of need, denial, compromise, and gratification.

Turning our attention inward, we may witness an inner world as busy and contradictory as what we see in the outer world. Might it be useful to ask ourselves what is commanding us, what is driving us at such speeds to so many diverse, contradictory, and individual ends?

The Compulsive Self

Help this headstrong self disintegrate;
That beneath it you may discover unity,
like a buried treasure.

Mathnawi I, 683

We are looking in the mirror again, trying to see ourselves as we actually are. Within every human being is a complex of drives, desires, self-doubts, and self-justifications that bolster our sense of identity and distinguish us from others. Put another way, a remarkable egoism has been incorporated into each one of us, the significance of which can hardly be overestimated.

The *compulsive self* is a Sufi term for that state of the self in which egoism rules, in which there is little or no separation between the impulses and compulsions of the ego and one's everyday waking state. In other words, this is a state in which all of one's self is absorbed into desires, needs, or impulses. In such a state, "I" *am* my hunger, my happiness, or my anger. There really is no "I" present; there is only the feeling-state to which we give the name "I."

In the stage of the compulsive self, a person is identified with infantile desires, identifying happiness with pleasure. Unfortunately, many adults are not quite convinced that happiness is other than the indulgence of pleasure. Despite many painful experiences, we forget that indulging our desires is not a reliable path to happiness. Some eventually wind up in the blind alley of addiction.

The desires of the body, when indulged, are quickly satiated, unlike the pleasures of the soul, which grow and grow. Indulging our desires will likely lead to imbalance and ill health. It also results in all kinds of inner conflicts. Even in childhood our two greatest drives are the desires we feel and the need for approval and love from others, which often come into conflict. So, from an early age we live in the tension between individual desire and social correctness, between our own pleasure and the approval of others.

The state of the compulsive self is a driven state without inner spaciousness, without presence. There is only the need to do, to fill an emptiness, to be continually busy. This may also manifest as compulsive behaviors such as the need for attention. Sometimes it may manifest as the need to belittle others or to defend and justify oneself. One of its foremost manifestations is the need to control. It may manifest as programs for revolution or salvation. It may even manifest itself as the egoic agenda to take care of others.

What all of these states have in common is a fundamental insufficiency of *being*. Most of our attempts to change our states and all systems of human development that work only to change our states—replacing negative ones with positive ones, sadness with happiness, anger with forgiveness, and so forth—ignore the fundamental issue, namely, that there is no real "I" present; no significant and reliable capacity to observe, direct, and will but only a battle of states. Without a different kind of "I" there can only be this continuous, automatic, and unconscious succession of states, the sum total of which assumes itself as "I."

A New Quality of "I-ness"

Prophets, messengers, and saints have been in this world trying to tell us that we are not as we think we are. We are not murky or muddy beings; we are essentially the purest water from the purest Source. We do not need to live in fear or guilt or as a slave to desires. We can live in joy, gratitude, and trust because we are the creation of Infinite Love. The purpose of that love is to be known and the purpose of our lives is to know this and express it.

Spiritual development is fundamentally the awakening of the core of ourselves, a point of consciousness and will. It is that point of consciousness that can truly be called "I." And yet it is an "I" that does not depend on a personal story, a résumé, a social role. It is this "I" that is the true source of human will and goodness. Without it we are merely, for better or worse, the sum of our contradictory compulsions and conditioning.

The core work of spirituality, and of healthy human development in general, is to transform this compulsive ego into a conscious presence. Since it would neither be possible nor desirable to live, relate, and function for long in this world without some sense of "I," the task is to bring about a new and different quality of "I-ness."

> The soul was made glad by that I-ness without "I"
> and sprang away from the I-ness of the world.
> Since it has been delivered from I, it has now become I:
> blessings on the "I" that is without affliction—
> for it is fleeing from its unreal I-ness
> and the real I-ness is running after it,
> since it saw the soul to be selfless.
> If you seek the real I-ness, it will not become a seeker of you:
> only when you have died to self
> will that which you seek seek you.
> If you are living, how should the corpse-washer cleanse you?
> If you are seeking,
> how should that which you seek go in search of you?
>
> *Mathnawi* V, 4139–43

When our sense of I-ness flows from a connection with Spirit, we are living at a different level of reality. Instead of the counterfeit self and its distorted perceptions, the soul is present with all the higher spiritual faculties of the heart. That ego that had been a tyrant over the heart has been transformed into a servant of the heart.

Every spiritual attainment is a victory over oneself. At the same time, it is the realization of our innermost nature. The transformation of the compulsive self is the transformation of the many egoistic tendencies through contact with the spiritual resources within our own essence.

The fragmented and incoherent self does its best to maintain a specious sense of control. Sailing upon an unpredictable ocean of often unrecognized and unacknowledged forces, it is like a fragile ship. All that we compulsively do to equip, maintain, tighten, and protect this fragile ship has no effect on the ocean. All of our restlessness and anxious seeking within the ship of our personality may be inadequate, mistaken, and superfluous, especially if we remain ignorant of the ocean.

Yet we are more than the captain of our own vessel; we have an unsuspected relationship with the wide and deep ocean itself. The ship, after all, was just a pretext to set sail upon the ocean.

At this stage, we may find ourselves confronting new questions. Can the ego overcome the ego? Can ego-driven thoughts and emotions clear away the ego's own ignorance? As Rumi writes in *Mathnawi* I, 3221–24: "Can the water of a polluted stream clear out the dung? How does a sword fashion its own hilt? Given our near powerlessness, where do we turn, and what can we do?"

The Holographic Principle, the Secret Within

What all human beings are seeking, the secret within material existence, is a force waiting to be discovered. It is the force that on a thorny branch produces a bud. It is the same force that transforms black coal into a clear diamond. It is the yearning that causes us to search deep within ourselves to find authentic being. This same force can renovate the human heart until it is a mirror reflecting the Infinite.

Abundance is seeking the beggars and the poor,
just as beauty seeks a mirror.
. . . . .

Beggars, then, are the mirrors of God's bounty,
and they that are with God are united with
Absolute Abundance.

Mathnawi I, 2745, 2750

We are the "poor" in relation to Absolute Abundance. We are also mirrors, reflectors of that abundance and all its qualities. Our purpose as mirrors is to manifest those qualities in our actions and relationships.

Or to put it another way: Within ourselves, in our core, is a power, a sacred impulse, a holographic sample of the Infinite, that is waiting to be purified and focused. Left unfocused, undirected, and unrefined, it will be absorbed into the chaotic desires of personal egoism and societal conditioning. Without a harmonizing higher influence, it will reflect the random conditioning of our environment. If we misuse this gift, we may harm others and ourselves.

One of the many ways the holographic essence is brought into everyday life is *adab*, spiritual courtesy. On the Sufi path, spiritual courtesy is one of the most valued practices, an antidote to the chaotic and egoistic behaviors that characterize more and more of modern life. As Rumi says,

Whoever lacks courtesy doesn't harm himself alone;
he sets fire to the whole world.

Mathnawi I, 79

Whenever we unconsciously follow our random and chaotic desires, we add to the burden of our negative conditioning, increasing the debt of our existence. The false self, when given free rein, is like a cruel camel driver, and the heart is the camel. A moment's weakness can lead us to entanglements and unforeseen consequences. Rumi says,

When, with just a taste,
envy and deceit arise,
and ignorance and forgetfulness are born,
know you have tasted the unlawful.

Mathnawi I, 1645

From a single taste of the forbidden fruit, envy and deceit arise.

At first an ill-chosen desire is like a small snake, relatively easy to pin down and subdue. But if repetitively indulged, it can become a fire-breathing dragon, assuming a commanding position in our lives.

If we are easily dominated by every impulse that arises, even water can turn to fire and burn us. But if our egos are educated to follow a deeper, purer course, we will reinforce the tendency toward freedom and the development of our spiritual nature. For anyone who cultivates conscious choice and conscious sacrifice, even fire may become like water.

The spiritual path corners the ego, uproots desires, bewilders the self-centered mind, deconstructs the false self. Sometimes the spiritual process, following its own mysterious wisdom, incapacitates the body before it rebuilds and restores it better than before.

Once the self is restored to sufficient health, the spiritual path asks of us a habit of moderate sacrifice and healthy self-denial. "Sleep less, eat less, speak less" is a maxim that applies more and more as the soul develops.

Little by little, spiritual practice restores the centrality of that conscious, witnessing, self-less center. Paradoxically, the soul becomes more capable of deep relationship—with others, with all of creation, and at the same time with an infinite, generous, and compassionate Reality.

5

Human Weakness, Cosmic Mercy

ANYONE WHO PROCEEDS A CERTAIN DISTANCE on the way of spiritual development will become increasingly aware of their faults. Some may even allow this awareness of weakness to banish them from God's presence. Yet it would be a mistake to let this emotional honesty become a source of discouragement. On the contrary, the acknowledgment of our weaknesses, backsliding, and heedlessness is itself a sign of increasing maturity.

It is the less mature, the less aware, who are blind to their own flaws, which, if they are glimpsed at all, tend to get obscured through self-justification and rationalization. These are people who have little or no taste for devotion and who imagine themselves to be quite autonomous. They may intend to do some good, but when the moment arrives, they get dissuaded or distracted; they fail to follow through with their intentions or fulfill their promises, often offering some excuse or rationalization as to why they will get to it later. These people believe they are exercising their own will, but what they think is their will is merely acting in their own self-interest. Real will is, in fact, almost nonexistent. They cannot activate their will apart from personal desire; in other words, they cannot activate a will that goes beyond their immediate self-interest.

Those of us who see these same tendencies in ourselves and honestly acknowledge them, realizing that we are somewhat helpless when confined to the ego's operating system, enter a wider context of awareness. Facing these faults in ourselves from a vantage point of presence is an important step in the process of self-knowledge and transformation.

The true gnostics[1] do not berate others for their weaknesses and mistakes, for they have seen the same in themselves. And it has taught them a deeper reliance on God. It is the gnostics who are enlivened by faith in such a way that the awareness of human imperfection becomes for them a reminder of Divine Mercy and Generosity. It is their expanded consciousness that allows a transcendent perspective and energy to transform the attributes of human nature. It is the awakened human being who is most capable of bringing spiritual insight to their faults. As the fourteenth-century Sufi master Ibn Abbad of Ronda says, "The servant's intimate knowledge of his spiritual states in discerning the good from the evil, and the relatively good from the relatively evil, is one of the rarest and most important kinds of knowledge. There is very little market for it these days."[2]

The Sufi mystics offer a twofold method for examining our faults. The first is to see our faults and mistakes and acknowledge the opportunity in them: in and of ourselves we are faulty and weak and in need of some higher force to be transformed.

Human nature is created from Truth (*Haqq*). Our potential for virtue and our potential to fall are inherent in our free will. The human being is the theater of Divine manifestation and free will is part of the story.

The second phase of the method is to humbly repent and ask for help in dealing with our shortcomings. We do not condone them, but we accept the situation we find ourselves in as necessary for our own process of awakening.

The first phase does not call for any judgment of ourselves, for we are the recipients of our own specific nature. In the second phase, we experience some sadness and regret for our condition. Conscience awakens. We acknowledge our "spiritual poverty" in relation to the Infinite. If we can do this, we will open ourselves to an inflow of grace, support, and guidance; our worldly passions and distraction will lessen; and our perception of true beauty will increase.

The alternative is to either become numb and oblivious to our faults or live in a state of anxiety about them. If we choose the former path of numbness and blindness, we are on a descending course, moving from truth to delusion, until sooner or later we encounter the immovable wall of actuality.

If we choose the second path of anxiety over our faults, we will detest ourselves and increasingly suffer from our own dissipation, but without the experience of grace, support, and guidance.

There may seem to be many reasons to suffer anxiety. We are continually faced with disappointments and challenges. Perhaps we notice how we either get stuck to the first negative thought that comes to our mind and slide further into negativity, or we see every form of deprivation as an opportunity, a reminder of the generosity and mercy of Being. Every deprivation then becomes something that opens the door to understanding and appreciation. As we consciously witness life's decrees and qualities within the theater of our own experience, we will find ourselves renewed. We will call to mind the prophets and saints—their examples of patience, contentment, humility, trust, gratitude, courage, and love.

Connecting with the Essence of Mercy

There is a hadith in which the Prophet Muhammad says that this tendency to "stray" is within all of us and how that tendency may be brought to surrender. He describes the support that was felt and the surrender that was the means to transform his "satan":

> "Every human being has the devil within. It flows like blood in the veins of man."
>
> "Even you, O Prophet?"
>
> "Yes, even me, although God has supported me and my satan (egoism) has surrendered."[3]

Some of us know too well how to be independent, at times excessively independent, even rebellious. This independent streak may impel us on this spiritual journey and yet possibly mislead us. At times, no doubt, we wander off the "straight path," while sometimes we find ourselves guided back to a new understanding of what that path is. Truth in its inexhaustible mercy sometimes allows us to go astray in order that going astray might be the cause of our returning. Human free will has many purposes.

Companionship of the Holy

Adam, the original human being, is the model for what a human being essentially is. In the Qur'anic narrative, Allah created Adam from water and clay and breathed Spirit into him. Then Allah asked the angels to bow down to Adam, and so they did, except for Iblis (Diablo), who refused, saying, "He is created from earth, while I am of fire, and besides, I can see that he is going to create great mischief." Then Allah says, "I know what you do not," and he asks the angels to name various phenomena and all they can do is say, "We only know what you tell us." But Adam, when asked to name things, has the mysterious power to name everything in existence! The Divine had bestowed Its own names—that is, spiritual attributes—within the very nature of Adam, the primordial human being. And so they remain to this day, in latency, waiting to be fully activated through the potential we all have to awaken and embody these qualities.

Adam was the eye of the Eternal, but he stumbled. He took one step into the dense world without conscious precaution. His "sin" may have been as slight as a hair, yet even an eyelash in the eye can blind us and be as great an obstacle to sight as a mountain.

If Adam and Eve had been able to take counsel with a wise guide, they might not have fallen, uttered their excuses and self-justifications, but Adam and Eve had to make this mistake and learn from it. They were alone, without spiritual elders.

When one mere ego is associated with another ego, our own intelligence becomes veiled, idle, and dangerous. But when another intellect is joined with our intellect, it can sometimes save us from our own mistakes.

The faithful are mirrors of the faithful. This is how their faces become clean. If intelligence is paired with another intelligence, light increases and the way becomes clear. But if one lost soul plots with another lost soul, darkness increases and they become more lost.

One laughing pomegranate
brings the whole garden to life.
Keeping the company of the holy
makes you one of them.
Whether you are stone or marble,
you will become a jewel
when you reach a human being of heart.

Plant the love of the holy ones within your soul;
don't give your heart to anything
but the love of those whose hearts are glad.
Don't go to the neighborhood of despair:
there is hope.
Don't go in the direction of darkness:
suns exist.

The heart guides you to the neighborhood of the saints;
the body takes you to the prison of water and earth.
Give your heart the food of holy friends,
seek maturity from those who have matured.

Mathnawi I, 717–26

An adage of the Sufi path says, "Find the friend of God: when you have done so, God is your friend."

Can the water of a polluted stream
clear out the dung?
Can human knowledge sweep away
the ignorance of the sensual self?
How does a sword fashion its own hilt?
Go, entrust the cure of this wound to a surgeon,
for flies will gather around the wound
until it can't be seen.
These are your selfish thoughts
and all you dream of owning.
The wound is your own dark hole.

Mathnawi I, 3221–24

But human weakness may sometimes have a benefit that virtue does not have. Ibn `Ata'llah, a thirteenth-century Sufi sage, has said, "It may be that He will open the door of obedience without opening the door of acceptance; or perhaps He will ordain sinfulness for you and make it a means to come to Him."

Some might suggest that this approach is too easy and may cause people to lessen their moral striving. But, on the contrary, getting too upset over the state of our souls can lead to a sense of hopelessness and depression. It causes us to focus too much on ourselves and not enough on the light. Some who have been raised in the "religion of fear" become so preoccupied with their own "sin" that they become alienated from the One they claim to worship. Too much contrition cuts us off from a perception of beauty and the awareness of mercy, whereas this continuous humble reliance on God can increase our certainty and become a better means to restraint and virtue than the fear of punishment alone.

The Prophet Muhammad said, "By the one who holds my soul in His hand, even if you did not sin, God would make of you a people who would sin and ask His forgiveness, so that you and He would have the pleasure of experiencing His forgiveness."

At the heart of the Sufi path is the Qur'an and the character of

Muhammad. The teachings come alive when we experience them as a means for reaching our true well-being. The practices are not a rigid set of external forms commanded by God but a means for learning how to surrender and be in harmony with the deep law of life. Each of the primary practices—ritual prayer, fasting, charity, pilgrimage, remembrance, service, and *adab* (spiritual courtesy)—is a way of transforming the ego from tyrant to servant, receiving grace, and connecting with the Infinite.

The ritual prayer teaches us to awaken within the flow of time and pay reverence to our Source. Fasting teaches the body to be patient and listen to a deeper call beyond the urgings of bodily hunger. Pilgrimage teaches us to take account of our life and trust in wayfaring. Charity teaches us to share and trust in Providence for our sustenance. Remembrance teaches the heart-mind to be continually grateful and aware. Service helps us to put aside our preoccupation with ourselves, to be free of the coercions of the ego. Adab teaches us the qualities of humility, gentleness, and respect. All of these teach the body, intellect, emotions, and soul to be in alignment and attunement with a higher truth.

This path is not only rooted in revelation and the example of the Prophet; many great human beings have walked it, too, and left us their accounts and insights. On the path of Sufism, we hope to learn from all the prophets, and from the *awliya*, the saints, the true friends of God. Ibn Abbad ar-Ronda offers this advice to spiritual seekers on the path of Sufism:

> They endeavor to make Him their companion in all their states, as far as they are able. He is merciful to them by causing them to no longer attend to their own weakness or strength in whatever they undertake or leave aside. Instead He is their safeguard and protection. . . . The difficult becomes easy and the harsh becomes bearable for these servants. God makes their every moment precious and most significant. He establishes them in comfort and in a great kingdom. In Him alone do they move or take their rest;

on Him alone do they rely; to Him alone do they raise all their thoughts and aspirations. That is why this community is preeminent among communities.[4]

As I witness this path unfolding, this teaching that keeps changing, deepening, and transforming, I also come to sense the possibility of opening to a source of guidance found within, yet beyond, myself. It is a path of guidance, deeply coherent because it is revealed from the heart of reality. It speaks to my deepest understanding because it is based in the deepest laws of life.

Taking Every Circumstance of Life as a Teaching

To trust enough to take every circumstance as a teaching is to become aware, on one level, of how little we trust, how the ego causes us problems. It's a bit like having a dog. We know that a dog can be "man's best friend." On the other hand, if the dog is not trained, if it barks at the wrong time, jumps all over your guests, isn't housetrained, or cannot be trusted, we will have problems. So on this path we take every circumstance of life as an opportunity to train the dog of our *nafs al ammara*.[5]

This *nafs* (ego) is worse than a disobedient pet: it gets invested in things and interferes with the flow of life. The ego worships the gods of immediate satisfaction, pleasure, status, and power. Through the ego's melodrama of suffering we witness its attachments. We should learn to distinguish this form of suffering from the suffering of the heart. The heart suffers when it sees love and friendship denied. But the ego's suffering is from taking things personally; worrying about self-image; perceptions of self-importance; identification with group, race, nationality, or even religion—all of which can be mere extensions of our own ego.

In observing the suffering ego, we may also notice that we have made our lives very complicated. So many of our actions are done for the sake of something else. We all have innate talents, the fulfillment of which brings us joy. But we also have emotional needs and worldly desires that become additional and unnecessary factors in the equation. For instance, a child has a gift for art and eventually learns that the world will pay money for art. But in order to be paid for art, one must produce it in a certain way, present oneself in a certain way, please the people who control the art market, follow trends, compete with other artists, et cetera, et cetera. This exposes one to a web of expectations, strategies, disappointments, pretensions, and ambitions, all of which have little to do with the innate joy of art.

Faithlessness is to get caught in trying to satisfy all the ego's contradictory desires. Faithlessness is to take life as an end in itself and to forget that there is a greater reality behind the circumstances and immediate satisfactions of life.

It is the tendency of the lower self to make life, and even the spiritual path, into an arena for its own entertainment and ambition, an end that serves the ego alone. We want things to be the way we want them to be, both in our material life and even on the spiritual path. Instead of living in a state of perpetual service and surrender, the lower self is always trying to be in control. When the soul is committed to learning from every circumstance of life, the compulsions of the lower self are witnessed more clearly and the soul comes under the influence of something higher.

A person who lives with a spiritual aim will not be enslaved to countless random desires but will discriminate and evaluate on the basis of that spiritual aim: "Is this serving my lower self, or is this serving my spiritual aim? Is this leading toward more entanglement in false values, or is this leading me toward spiritual freedom and truth?" Even spiritual teachings need to be evaluated: Are they leading us toward subtle ego satisfactions, or are they purifying the self?

What the lower self needs to learn, however, is that this help and guidance is not to be found on the ego's own terms. In other words, when the ego proclaims, "I will learn what I want to learn, when I want to learn it, and in the way I want to learn it," it is actually shutting itself off from help and support of the Unseen. We have to ask ourselves honestly whether some of our activities might be a defense against becoming empty and opening ourselves to the transformative action of God.

Only when we are willing to become naked and empty before the Divine can we receive the inflow of *baraka*, the energy of grace, that we need for this spiritual journey. Only then will our own soul be magnetized by the help and grace that Being offers.

The kind of trust that is asked for here is not a blind trust but a conviction based on the awareness of our need and the understanding that help is available.

Tradition and the Grace of the Unseen

An authentic spiritual tradition is like a battery charging us from an unseen dimension. To connect oneself to that charge requires a certain emptying of self: letting go of one's preoccupations, agendas, and complexes. This rarely happens on one's own.

A spiritual community, a group of people who recognize a higher Source and who honor their own interdependence can become a vehicle for this higher energy and help. Through the rituals of worship, a group of people can become open and receptive to a degree that is difficult for an individual to attain. This is one reason why *tariqah*, the spiritual path, is not an individual tutorial but a communal undertaking. As part of a circle of lovers, we may attract the experiences and perceptions that support real faith.

The Gifts of Servanthood and Community

Spiritual community creates possibilities for the privilege of conscious service. Servanthood is an opportunity to lessen the preoccupation with our nafs, to enjoy the freedom of serving others without any expectation of reward or praise.

Rumi says quite clearly,

No one gains admittance to Him except through servanthood. "God lacks nothing, but you are needy" [*Surah al-Muhammad* 47:38]. It is not possible to say of a person who is granted admission to God that he is more closely related to God or better acquainted than you are. His access is easier only because of his servanthood.

Signs of the Unseen [Fihi ma fihi], Discourse 45

Many years ago, I met a young man who had come to Turkey all the way from Egypt and for weeks had been trying to help another who had fallen into some kind of legal trouble. He himself had very little money and was barely making ends meet.

"What is your relationship to him?" I asked.

"I hardly know him. We met briefly once. But he doesn't know anybody here, and I'm the one he asked for help."

Little did I know that this young man would eventually become a prodigious scholar of Islam. But I met him when he was a nobody helping another nobody.

God willing, to the extent that we begin to sense that there is a great, generous, and beautiful Being behind the veils of appearance, our taste for servanthood will increase.

Call Out in Your Need

Rumi says,

God is the Absolute Giver. He filled the lap of the sea with pearls; He coupled the thorn with the raiment of the rose; He bestowed life and spirit upon a handful of dust without ulterior motive and without precedent. All parts of the world have a share of Him.

When someone hears that in a certain city there is a generous person who engages in extreme liberality, he will certainly go there in hopes of gaining a share in that generosity. Since God's munificence is so well known, since all the world is aware of His grace and kindness, why don't you ask Him for a robe of honor and a purse? Instead you sit like a dunce and think that if He wants, He will give you something. You make no entreaty, while a dog, which has neither rational intelligence nor understanding, will come to you when it is hungry and wag its tail as if to say, "Give me something to eat. I have nothing to eat, but you do." This much discernment it has. You are not less than a dog that would not be content to sit in a dust heap and say, "If he wants, he will give me something to eat." No, a dog will beg and wag its tail. You too should "wag your tail" and beg God, for before such a benefactor, begging is what is required. If you are not blessed with good fortune, seek your fortune from Him who is not stingy and who is possessed of wealth. God is extremely close to you. Whatever idea or conceptualization of Him you may have, He is something like that because it is He who brings that concept or idea of yours into being and holds it up for you to see. However, He is too close for you to see Him. Why should this seem strange? In your every act your mind is not only with you but is the initiator of that act; yet you can't see your mind. Although you can see it through its effects, you can never see its essence.

—*Signs of the Unseen [Fihi ma fihi]*, Discourse 45

Though this world seems to be filled with a kind of light, the light of the senses, nevertheless we are in a kind of spiritual darkness unless we begin to see with that spiritual light.

Choosing a Path

Making that call to the Divine also means that we ourselves are called to a work of heroic proportions. Such a work as the spiritual journey can never occupy second place in our lives.

We should choose a path that is as complete as possible, one that can reconcile our human and our divine nature, not one that will remove us from life and other human beings, nor leave us stranded in an idealistic and impractical pseudo-enlightenment.

There are genuine spiritual paths within all the great sacred traditions. Throughout history, the Compassionate Intelligence has been communicating with humanity through prophets and sacred books, through enlightened beings and the paths they walked. And, of course, human beings have been complicating and obscuring the essential message almost as quickly as it was received. Nevertheless, the great sacred traditions have become the enduring repository of inspiration and collective human wisdom.

A genuine spiritual path recognizes both the generosity of grace and the need for individual human effort. On the one hand, the Source that created us is incredibly abundant and loving. It is capable of delivering us from our own confusion and weakness. On the other hand, it is our responsibility to clear away the obstacles, and remove the rust from the mirror of the heart, and continually orient ourselves by means of the best principles and noblest values. Assuming responsibility for ourselves will begin with wresting attention from trivialities and distractions, and reconnecting it with the soul. Then attention will be the light the soul casts on existence.

6

Attention and Our Inner Being

... people who remember God standing, and sitting,
and lying on their sides ...

Qur'an, *Surah al `Imran* 3:191

HOW OFTEN HAVE I HEARD this extraordinary verse quoted by
Sufis, offered as an example of the importance of remembering
God in every circumstance of life. But as I was working on this chapter, I became curious about the context of this verse. Will most know
who exactly it is referring to? Those endowed with insight remember
God standing, and sitting, and lying on their sides, and contemplate
the creation of the heavens and the earth. This perpetual state of remembrance and contemplation is the attribute and consciousness of
those who possess "insight," literally the "kernel" of meaning. And
this leads them to contemplate the creation of the heavens and the
earth. And in the following verse it is asserted: "O our Sustainer! You
have not created any of this without meaning and purpose. Limitless
are You in Your Glory. Deliver us from the anguish of the Fire."

These few verses describe a human potential. A progression of
meanings is revealed: Those who possess the kernel of insight find
themselves remembering God in different states, and through this
they are led to contemplate manifest creation and discover that everything serves a purpose.

In the previous chapter we considered the interdependent nature of human weakness and imperfection and its relationship to spiritual grace. Our natural imperfection and incompleteness is remedied through the influences of a higher order of reality.

But why is it that we are so rarely like those who remember "standing, and sitting, and lying on [our] sides"? Why is this not our natural condition? Is there something to be done? A work of the soul? And is this work of the soul even possible within the conditions of contemporary life?

Part of the discipline of the dervish[1] is to be always aware of the difference between life lived in the everyday state of heedlessness (*ghaflah*) and life lived with presence (*hudhur*), the quality of attention that requires a subtle awakening. The reasons for our heedlessness are many, but the remedy lies in understanding the nature of attention. In order to understand this sleeping state and the mechanism that perpetuates it, we need to study attention.

> Normally, we are what holds our attention.
> O friend, you are what you think.
> As for the rest of you, it's only flesh and bone.
> If your thought is a rose, you are a rose garden;
> and if your thoughts are thorns,
> you are just kindling for the bath stove.
>
> *Mathnawi* II, 277–78

Until we are in a state of conscious presence, we are merely whatever commands and occupies our attention. We want to keep "the rose" in mind, but our minds are drawn to judgment, worry, regret, discontent, desire.

Passive attention merely reacts to whatever is strongest in our environment, especially whatever threatens or exalts our ego. As long as our attention is identified with our ego, it will always be reactive. But if we can train our attention to focus on our values, on our highest understanding, then our attention becomes the ally and servant of our heart and soul.

Remembrance of the Divine Name is a simple and effective way to bring our egos, minds, and hearts into an alignment with a higher-order reality. For Rumi, Allah is the essential name that comprises all the attributes and represents the unified field. As such, this essential name of God is the satisfier of every need, the remedy for every ill.

So why do we need a whole book such as this? Because our thoughts and desires too easily command our attention, complicate our psyches, and waylay us from this simple truth.

It is every human being's responsibility to acquire true knowledge about the nature of our souls and the spiritual milieu in which we exist. Rumi refers to such knowledge as "the Sciences of Wisdom":

> The Sciences of Wisdom are God's armies,
>   by which He strengthens the spirits of the initiates
> and purifies their knowledge from the adulteration of ignorance,
>   their justice from the adulteration of bias,
> their generosity from the adulteration of ostentation,
> and their forbearance from the adulteration of foolishness;
> and brings near to them whatever was far from them
> in their understanding of the hereafter;
> and makes easy to them whatever was hard for them
> in respect of obedience and energetic endeavor.
> No one gains admittance to Him except through servanthood.
>   "God lacks nothing, but you are needy."
>
> *Mathnawi* III, Prologue

So, the "Sciences of Wisdom" are correctives for the distortions of egoism such as bias, ostentation, and foolishness. But we are getting ahead of ourselves, and we must look carefully at how attention functions in our lives.

Becoming Attention Rather Than Seeking Attention

The need for attention is a basic need in human beings. From childhood, every human being has a certain need for attention, and if we're deprived of it, we will develop strategies to gain it, even to steal it. This unconscious need for attention and various strategies for getting it is normal for children, but it is not befitting a mature adult. And yet whole careers and areas of human activity are built upon this need to gain the attention of others: fashion, athletic competition, rock and roll, and looking "holy," to randomly name a few.

Upon the foundation of that fundamental human need we build another structure from the need for approval. In our unconscious condition, in the state of sleep, we are habitually seeking to gain the approval of others and to avoid their disapproval. This need for approval is only tangentially linked to any sense of value or worthiness; rather, it is simply about approval and disapproval.

Given that society, and sometimes even the family structure, exists on a foundation of false or superficial values, this desire to gain the approval of others leads us further and further away from our inner being, our essential self. It can even lead to a state of hypocrisy if we abandon our own integrity merely to win the approval of others, especially those in authority.

On the spiritual path, however, we learn to observe ourselves, our reactions, our needs for approval and attention, our need to be "right," our wish to appear better than we are, and all the things the false self is built upon. To rigorously observe what we are doing to gain attention and approval requires that we awaken a witness in ourselves, an observer that is free from these needs. We hope to be selfless warriors, confronting our own hypocrisies, lessening the grip of our judgments and opinions.

In our heedlessness we live our lives expecting that there should be no resistance to our search for pleasure, no disturbance of our ego's expectations, no lack of approval from others. When we meet suffering, disturbance, the judgment of others, our immediate reaction is to either blame something outside ourselves or blame ourselves rather than simply witnessing as an objective and compassionate observer.

It is clear that when we are in this unconscious state of blaming or looking for something to blame, we are far from that witnessing consciousness that simply subsists in pure presence.

The esoteric path is about awakening our inner being, the essential self, that is free from the expectation of being continually undisturbed, or approved of by others, or receiving unvarying admiration from the world around us. The path is about cultivating inner conscience and sincerity.

Having recognized how much of our lives have been lived in a state of heedlessness, our attention merely being drawn to this or that, or merely reacting to events, we can now recognize the possibility of assuming responsibility for the precious substance of our attention.

When I can *become attention itself*, it feels as if attention is arising within and through myself and reaching out into the world connecting my very being with whatever I am giving my attention to. I may be noticing rain pouring from a cloud far in the distance over the ocean, or a tree branch waving in the wind. I am one with what I am observing and with myself simultaneously. I also realize that attention is to some extent under the control of my will. I can choose what to pay attention to, whether to focus on some details like the light dancing off the leaves of a tree or the state of my own being with its mixture of gratitude, thoughts of other people, slight apprehension about what I need to accomplish on this day—all held in a field of conscious attention.

When we become attention itself, we are disconnected from the distorting mechanism of egoism. We are freed from these unrealistic expectations of constant pleasure, approval, and nondisturbance. When we have become attention itself, we are in the state of presence and the soul is awake—and even when facing difficulty or loss, we are more spontaneously in harmony with the guidance and intelligence of Spirit.

And this is why, on the spiritual path, you will not be preached to. You will be encouraged to observe yourself in a nonreactive way; to study your reactions, judgments, and opinions, to not give them so much importance, and to rely instead on that deeper self that is not enslaved by the false values of the world, the unconscious needs for attention and approval, but a self that exists under the auspices of Divine Mercy and Compassion.

7

The Work of the Soul

THE WORD *SOUL* IN ENGLISH is a vague and slippery term. For some people, *soul* and *spirit* are interchangeable terms; some will even debate the definitions of each term against people who might say, "What you call spirit, I call soul," and vice versa.

In classical metaphysics, spirit (*pneuma*) is that vital principle that animates all life, while soul (*psyche*) is the spiritual part of a person that is eternal. The confusion around these words is one cause of the declining grasp of metaphysics in contemporary cultures.

In an earlier chapter we offered the following definition: within the context of Sufi metaphysics, "soul" can be understood as the result of the union of self and Spirit.

In Islam, Spirit is the primary manifestation of the Divine, something like "Holy Spirit" in Christianity. For an individual on the spiritual path, Spirit (*Ruh*) refers to that diamond-like infinite point of pure spiritual potential, accessible within us.

This definition is meant to describe a phenomenon that can be experienced rather than an unproven supernatural concept to be believed. A religious definition of *soul* might be "the eternal aspect of ourselves that will be either punished or rewarded in eternity." But the definition we're using has a practical purpose. It suggests that the self can more and more be brought into relationship with Spirit. If we picture a spectrum of experience with egoism (selfish and unconscious) at one end and soul (loving and perceptive) at the other, we can imagine for ourselves what it might feel like when we are more or less soul-full or . . . *soul-less*.

As the self gradually becomes more and more infused with Spirit, the quality of the self is transformed. The relationship of self and Spirit is cultivated in many ways, but what is essential is the awareness of something beyond the ego-self. Soul is what our inner being feels like when Spirit is the active force and the self is receptive to it. Then our attention is guided by Spirit rather than merely reacting to circumstance.

But when the self persists in denial (*kufr*) of Spirit, taking its own desires as its gods, the soul-less self is vainly trying to be in control and satisfy its many cravings.

When our sense of self is confined to the prison of the ego's habits and patterns, that self is, to a great extent, perpetuating its own misery. Rumi described egoism as "an inch-deep river in which we drown."

The more the self can be in attunement with Spirit, the more it can know the reality beyond the material world, beyond space and time. The soul is a knowing substance because the soul is infused with the intelligence of Spirit. This may sound like a remote possibility when we are overcome by the distractions and worries of our everyday lives. And yet it is verifiably true . . . if we can subtly lay aside the conditioned mind and embrace the unfolding of *what is* (*wujud*).

To acquire this kind of being is to become illuminated, to be connected to a greater Intelligence that will guide us step by step on the way. The developed soul, instead of living in fear and uncertainty, becomes more and more able to trust the unfolding of life.

The work of the soul, then, is the cultivation of presence and remembrance in resonance with the Mysterion at the core of our being. Presence includes all the ways we mindfully attend to our lives. Presence is a comprehensive self-awareness that simultaneously encompasses body, emotion, and thought. If presence is sustained sufficiently, we begin to notice that "our" presence is sourced in a greater Presence. This is the beginning of true remembrance. Remembrance is our awareness of that greater field of Being that sustains everything, including presence itself.

But before we can truly appreciate and encompass the vivifying and uplifting nature of Being, we have to deal with what takes us away from presence and remembrance. This is what we must observe in ourselves. Bear with me for a while, but we must get through this and understand the traps, games, and bad habits of the false self.

Deluded Motivations, False Strategies

Among the many I's, the false selves that make up our personal identity, or our "personality," all of them serve several basic motivations. Each motivation is determined by the wish to gain or avoid something that is believed to be good or bad, desirable or undesirable. The totality of these motivations, or urges, is called in some literature "the world" (*dunya*) or in the Bible, "mammon."

It is not the created world that is the problem but rather the loss of a spacious consciousness, a greater context, the sense of the sacred.

As we look at our lives in this particular cultural era, let's begin by acknowledging where many of us are. In the workaday world there are incredible demands made on us. We are a culture that has made an idol of "work" to such an extent that in this culture, more than in most, people are identified with their work, their positions, and their financial security. This enslavement to society's demands is rampant, out of perceived necessity and sometimes from misplaced ambitions.

We have to acknowledge how much our individualities are shaped by the demands of our "work" and the expectations of society around us. And yet we're searching for another way. How might it be possible to be as "those whom neither business nor profits distract from the remembrance of God" (*Surah an-Nur* 24:37)? We need to have an inner discipline to keep in balance, especially in these times with the pace of change accelerating and with the overwhelming bombardment of information and impressions.

And this is especially the case if our attention has been more or less completely focused on the external world, absorbed in what's "out there": how we're being treated by others, how we're being seen by others, how we're doing in our jobs, and so forth. The outer world can absorb almost all of our attention. Our thoughts and emotions are all about what is happening in our outer lives. We are engaged with this outer world in an uncontrollable state, consisting in various proportions of fears, insecurities, resentments, disappointments, regrets, and conflicting desires, the totality of which we can never resolve nor bring into a bearable order.

Internally we may see that we've been like someone whose whole life has been spent looking at a television screen, except that we don't have any control over what channel we're watching and what advertisements we're forced to listen to. All of this "noise" is just there, and we cannot separate from it. We're identified with the contents of our psyche that we take to be ourselves. The connection to the inner stillness of the soul is absent.

So this is the human situation and increasingly so in this contemporary, more or less Godless outer world that we live and work in. And even among the "religious" who really do their best to live their faith and a moral life, this awareness of the core of inner being often seems to be lacking.

In my book *Living Presence*, I describe a threefold process involving deconditioning, reconditioning, and unconditioning.

The process of deconditioning involves reducing the noise, the static, the distortions within the mind. Although different types of people are conditioned in different ways, the common thread consists in the compulsions and coercions of the false self: vanity, pride, envy, resentment, to name a few. We can add to the list all feelings of grievance, being "owed" and "if only . . ." All these forms of negativity are imaginary problems that arise from the very nature of the false self.

The study, observation, and disarming of the false self is a vast subject. There are many approaches that might be taken. Rumi's immense wisdom illuminates so many of the problematic areas of human life. The primary sources of Islam, the Qur'an and hadiths,[1] provide essential guidance for living a sane and conscious life. Other wisdom traditions may also be sources of effective knowledge.

A Methodology for Deconditioning the Self

Some suffering is inevitable in our lives, but then there is the suffering we unconsciously create for ourselves. The following model has been developed from insights learned from Dr. Robert Gibson,[2] a little-known but wise spiritual teacher of the twentieth century.

If we were to objectively observe what causes most of our suffering, we would see that we unconsciously live under a great delusion: *we have convinced ourselves that the primary purpose of living is to seek as much as possible to be undisturbed.* This assumption is the foundation of our inner slavery.

This delusion is sustained by seven basic motivations:

1. To preserve our own existence at any cost
2. To gain pleasure and comfort, to escape all pain
3. To gain attention, to avoid being ignored or rejected
4. To gain approval, to escape disapproval
5. To gain a sense of importance, to escape the sense of inferiority
6. To be loved (or at least needed), and to avoid being abandoned
7. To have control over other people, and to escape situations we cannot control

All of these are natural, even healthy motivations in appropriate circumstances and in due proportions. When we live with acceptance and trust, as any true spiritual teaching would encourage, we may have our preferences, likes and dislikes, but we do not make them all-important. A problem arises if we seek above all to try to maintain the delusion of "being always undisturbed." It is then that these motivations can become immoral, even depraved, and lead us into exploitation, stealing, deception, and hypocrisy.

As we try to reach this imaginary "undisturbed" state, we have several primary strategies that we may employ, each of which is a symptom of an unhealthy mental state:

1. *Complaining.* This hasn't worked so far and merely perpetuates a state of resentment.
2. *Playing the "victim" and demanding our rights.* This hasn't worked so well, either, especially if it entails an avoidance of personal responsibility.
3. *Adopting a "mask" to please people.* Even if this sometimes works temporarily, it creates inner havoc through the abandonment of our true needs.
4. *Trying to conform and do as one is told by "authorities."* This opens the door to personal and mass suggestibility and the forfeiting of integrity and authenticity.
5. *Blaming, shifting responsibility for our state to something external to ourselves.* When something seems to go wrong and we feel irritated, angry, or bitter, we search for a "reason" to blame someone or something for the state we're in.

So, these are some of the primary motivations of the false self and the strategies it creates in its misguided attempts to reduce its self-created miseries. We probably did not invent these strategies; more likely we inherited them from the world around us and, especially in these times, various media that pitch themselves to the lowest common denominator of humanity, or worse, seek to manipulate us for hidden purposes.

The delusion of believing that the purpose of life is to be always undisturbed causes us to erect defenses and barriers of self-protection that only imprison us in the ego's own illusions. This posture of defiance represents a refusal to learn from life.

Escaping the Tyranny of the False Self

Ego and soul are different states of the same substance: our identity, our I-ness. Ego, however, might be understood as the "I" confined and distorted by the motivations and strategies just described. What is usually meant by "ego" is the "I" acting under such compulsions and strategies. The spiritual process begins with this work of deconditioning the ego-self and simultaneously reconditioning through presence, remembrance, and the knowledge of the soul.

An essential aspect of spiritual practice is a rigorous encounter with the ego's delusions. By rigorously cultivating self-awareness—a primary tool of spiritual work—we may see the many ways in which the ego ruins things for us.

Egoism is the most useless, good-for-nothing fraud ever perpetrated by and on ourselves. It begins as a pathetic attempt to impress others, to assert one's superiority. But just as self-praise is never flattering, self-assertion never hits its target. Only other self-deceived fools buy into the ego's self-promotion. In fact, the ego's strategies of self-defense only invite attack. The ego's strategies attempt to avoid reality, but obviously there is a price to pay for denying reality. In the end, the ego will prove to be its own worst enemy. The harm the ego does, it does mostly to itself.

If insanity is insisting on repeating a failed strategy again and again, the ego is not sane. The ego cannot win us love. Only selflessness removes the barriers to letting ourselves be loved.

True sanity begins in the disenchantment with the many ways the ego, or false self, tries to attain happiness. Whether the ego strives for material possessions, romantic satisfactions, or even religious piety, the very self-centered nature of its motivation exerts a negative influence and assures a negative outcome.

To take the path of Sufism is not to have "mystical" visions or ecstatic experiences, to withdraw from everyday life, or to try to become someone special. To be a Sufi is to be free of one's ego and live from the soul.

The most precious friend in this life is someone who is working to be free from their own ego's machinations, someone who sincerely prefers selflessness to self-importance, who prefers a merging harmony with others rather than domination over them. The best of friends are the people who have made their primary focus the work on their inner being, and the memory of such people seems to outlast the memory of conquerors and kings, the rich and powerful. In some cases, these explorers and heroes of the inner life have left behind records and maps, insights and spiritual practices that help us develop our souls.

The Invisibility of True Values

The more human beings are awakened to the soul, the more they will sacrifice their lives for love, for the well-being of others, for a transcendent reality they directly experience. Admittedly we also chase after illusions, whims, and desires, but we learn that the attainment of these does not bring meaningful peace or fulfillment.

If we were to analyze what is of lasting value, we would have to conclude that what we truly value is in an invisible dimension. Contentment is invisible. Peace is invisible. Integrity is invisible. Love and friendship are invisible. It does not matter that we have attained wealth or fame if the price of those things is inner conflict, remorse, disharmony, fear, regret, shame, or simply a shallow and superficial life. A life spent chasing after outer attainments at the expense of inner values proves to be a life wasted—the precious substance of life spent on the trivialities of the ego.

From a slightly different perspective, we can say that the purpose of life is a project of transforming ourselves into ever more complete and inwardly rich human beings. We are souls in progress, integrating into ourselves the invisible qualities and virtues of a spiritual reality that is our birthright.

Imagine the quality of our lives if we continually keep this purpose in mind. Each day becomes a work of spiritual creativity. We need not turn away from the world we find ourselves in but instead use every circumstance as an opportunity for developing our spiritual qualities. Rather than a strategy to satisfy more of our ever-arising desires for attention, pleasure, and control, we might instead cultivate inner freedom, purity of heart, humbleness, unselfish love, generosity, and courage. How different are the paths to outer power and accumulation, versus the path to dignity, presence, and intimacy.

There is a *hadith qudsi*: "(God says:) And when I love My servant, I become his hearing with which he hears, his eyes with which he sees, his hands with which he touches, and his feet with which he walks."

Our lives find meaning through a process of search and discovery made possible by the spiritual faculties with which we are endowed by the Mysterion. This is not a statement of belief or theology as much as a statement of life as it can be experienced. The simple fact is that the most significant, satisfying, and enduring experiences that we have are experiences of meaning found through relationships with other human beings, with ourselves, and ultimately with something much greater than ourselves.

Rumi represents this ever-deepening relationship between self and Spirit with this example:

A Beloved asks her lover: who do you love more—yourself or me? The lover answers: There's nothing left of me but my name. From my head to my toe I have become You.

This is not the absorption of one ego into another. It is the dissolving of both into a relationship based in Truth. When two (or more) people are capable of this, God is present. This is the realization of the age-old "Whenever two or more are gathered in my name, there am I" (Matthew 18:20).

There is another hadith qudsi: "(God says:) My love belongs by right to those who sit with one another in Me, who love one another in Me."

Choosing the Path of Awakening

The spiritual path (*tariqah*) is a path of awakening. It is an endeavor beyond the common preoccupations of the world, even beyond conventional religion and morality. It begins when a person realizes profoundly that something is missing, that "the world" with its superficial values, relationships, and ambitions will never in itself satisfy us.

The "dervish" has become aware of the futility and superficiality of life as it is commonly lived, including much of religion, politics, and worldly ambitions, and has chosen the path of awakening, which requires conscious intention. The seeker has come to see how much they have been perpetuating the state of sleep, and out of this realization comes a sincere wish to be more sensitive, more awake.

Increasingly the seeker becomes aware of two states of being, two ways of living. One is about trying to meet the ego's expectations, and the other is about listening to the heart. One is about desiring attention, and the other is about becoming attention.

Until we have experienced awakening and known how asleep we ourselves can be, we cannot know how deep is the sleep most human beings accept as the normal state of consciousness.

> Forgetfulness of God, beloved,
> is the support of this world;
> spiritual intelligence its ruin.
> For Intelligence belongs to that other world,
> and when it prevails, this material world is overthrown.
>
> *Mathnawi* I, 2066–67

This perception of the condition of humanity is not elitism. In this view there is no judging others as inferior and imagining oneself to be superior. That would be just another aspect of this state of sleep we are referring to. The presence of the soul is beyond such judging.

Soul, the Mediator of True Knowledge

The soul is the mediator of true knowledge because what we mean by knowledge is not something assembled deductively from below but something that is given from "above," from a higher order of reality.

Knowledge is the seal of the kingdom of Solomon—
the whole world is form, and knowledge is the life-giving spirit.

Mathnawi I, 1030

Solomon's "seal" includes the knowledge of spiritual laws and proportions, sacred geometry, understanding the "languages" of nature, harnessing of unseen forces, and, symbolically, the building of the temple.

An important function of the soul's knowledge is that it enlivens material form with Spirit. Form is enlivened, animated, and fulfilled by the soul's knowledge. The saints and prophets are those who make a lasting contribution to civilization and humanity through new forms of art, literature, music, architecture, and society, above all by indicating and embodying the work of the soul.

In later chapters we will explore spiritual perception, discernment, and intelligence and how these are essential to the work of the soul. But next we will consider how love is the ultimate explanation of everything!

8

The Way of Love

I F YOU HAVE EVER FALLEN COMPLETELY IN LOVE, you know we
come alive when we are in love. In the state called "falling in love,"
two people give the substance of attention to each other in such a way
that each one feels valued and, even more significantly, *recognized*.
In the state of giving and receiving love, we feel more alive and all
of life takes on the glow of love. Lovers listen deeply to each other;
they hear each other's every word. It is such an intense experience
that people can even become addicted to it.

As beautiful as this is, however, it is not the most mature, enduring, or beautiful love. But it does reveal to us the power of love to
bring happiness, to enliven and transform.

Instead of the fleeting highs of love, is it possible to know a more
enduring, constant, and true love? It is difficult enough to find it and
sustain it with one person. How can we love in widening circles of human beings? Ultimately, how might we love the Source of Life Itself?

These may seem like very exalted and idealistic questions, given
the lives that many of us face day by day. I don't know if I would have
even been interested in such questions before I had a certain extraordinary experience of love. It did not come through my high school
sweetheart. It did not come, at first, through any romantic relationship. To my astonishment it came through a simple grandfather-like
man from Turkey in whose presence I felt immediately accepted and
loved. But it was not a love that felt personal; it wasn't about *me*. It
was as if I found myself, quite unexpectedly, in a different universe—

Love's universe. Though this was my first experience of this unprecedented kind of love, it was not my only experience of it. It was to be repeated in varying degrees among those who had been "cooked" in the kitchens of the Sufi tradition.

In What Sense Is Love a "Path"?

The answer lies in understanding the cosmic context in which we exist—namely, that we live in a universe of Love. Not only is God Love, as it has so often been said, but Love is literally both the cause and the purpose of all existence.

> Love is the path and direction of our Prophet.
> We are born from Love; Love is our mother.
> O Mother, hidden behind the body's veil,
> Concealed by our own cynical nature.
>
> Quatrain 57

Love is a fundamental cosmic energy, analogous to electricity, that can be tapped and used in many ways. In fact, one of my teachers said, "You are going to learn how to plug yourself into the outlet of Cosmic Love. The vast universe was created from just a spark of Love." Love is the cause insofar as it is an expression of the creative power that brought everything into existence. It is the purpose of existence, insofar as all of existence is revealing the qualities of Love. In other words, the most urgent fact of existence may be this: *Love loves to make Itself known to us.*

The discussion and exploration of love is simultaneously intellectual, emotional, psychological, and spiritual. It is ultimately spiritual, because love is profoundly related to the nature of reality itself. To explore the nature of love is to understand our absolute need for it, its relationship to beauty, its power to awaken new perceptions, its transformative effect on us, and ultimately how it leads to a perception of Truth Itself.

Spiritual love has a cognitive function: it transforms perception. The world looks different to a lover:

> To the Prophet, this world is plunged in glorification of God,
> while to us it is heedless.
> To his eye this world is filled with abundant love;
> to the eyes of others it is inert and lifeless.
> To his eye, valley and hill are in fluid motion:
> he hears subtle discourses from sod and bricks.
> To the vulgar, this whole world is a dead thing in chains:
> I have never seen a veil of blindness more amazing than this.
>
> *Mathnawi* IV, 3532–35

There are many levels to this experience of love. Love makes possible a transformation of perception and being, because love is itself the highest truth, the nature of reality. When we are more in the state of self-less love, we are closer to the truth, therefore our perceptions are spot-on.

Love is an elixir, the greatest transforming power in existence.

> By love, the bitter becomes sweet;
> by love, copper becomes gold;
> by love, the dregs become clear;
> by love, the dead become living;
> by love, the king becomes a slave.
> From knowledge, love grows.
> Has stupidity ever earned someone such a throne?
>
> *Mathnawi* II, 1529–32

Love Is a Fire and Ego Is Its Fuel

While there are many explanations of love, I would like to propose this one: Conscious love is the degree of relationship between the human lover and the Divine Beloved. You see, this is another aspect of creating soul, the communion between self and Spirit. And if this relationship between lover (self) and Beloved (Spirit) is encouraged to fulfill itself, it will result in harmony, communion, and even union.

But before we go there, we should be reminded of what stands in the way of love—namely, egoism, by which I mean all the motivations, strategies, and defenses of the false self that were described in the previous chapter. Negativity, blaming, and judgment are like filters that color and distort what we see. Fear, suspicion, or lust affect how we see others.

Such negative states are like shadows that vanish when the light of real love appears. When we can see and recognize another human being with the eyes of love, we not only free ourselves from distorted perceptions but we help to transform the other person as well.

When recognized by love, people are more likely to take off their masks. This may be why we feel more ourselves in the presence of a holiness that doesn't judge or blame. The holiest beings I have ever known were the least judgmental. They were like polished mirrors; they simply reflected back what was in front of them. In the presence of such people, we do not feel judged, though we might feel something awesome and humbling that inspires us to strive to be worthy of that love.

To be worthy of that love is not to destroy a sense of "I." Without some sense of identity we could not relate or function. We could not be in a relationship of love. Instead, the task is to purify the sense of I-ness. If we can rid the false self of its distortions, prejudices, vanity, self-righteousness, defensiveness, and unreasonable fears, we would be left with a wholly different sense of self. Rumi has a very interesting proposal for how to deal with our egoism and negativity:

My soul is a furnace
happy with the fire.
Love, too, is a furnace,
and egoism is its fuel.

    Mathnawi II, 1376–77

The conscious soul is itself a fiery furnace that burns up and consumes the negative traits of egoism. The soul of the lover can be a furnace energized and sustained by the infinite power of Spirit, a fire that can be both subtle and fierce.

All of the pathologies of egoism deserve to be thrown into the fire. The many-headed Hydra of false I's will have to die, but that dying is a miraculous sacrifice.

> For lovers, there is a dying in every moment:
> truly, the dying of lovers is not of one kind.
> The lover has been given two hundred lives
> from the Soul of Guidance;
> each instant she sacrifices another.
> For each life she gives, she receives ten:
> as it is said in the Qur'an, "Ten like unto them" (*Surah Hud* 11:13).
>
> —*Mathnawi* III, 3834–35

But the fire of love is not the only corrective for the pathologies of egoism. The gentler remedial power is *presence*, that state of comprehensive self-awareness that encompasses thought, emotion, sense impressions, and bodily activity.

Presence is also the awakened consciousness that inherently reflects the cosmic field of love. Presence is the portal through which we enter the field of conscious life. Just by being present with an open heart, we can enter into the cosmic milieu of love in which the false I's are more likely to dissolve. We can stop defending these false I's by dissolving the resentment and defensiveness that underlies them. What has to die is not a sense of self but the rationalizations and justifications that create and defend the false self.

Furthermore, when we no longer sustain the blame and judgment that sustain the false self, we will enter a pragmatic humility. This humility is not having a low estimate of ourselves. Humility is our awareness of our dependence on the cosmic field of love. In other words, humility is our awareness of our dependence on and need for "God."

The Way of the Lover

As I reflect on what set me on the spiritual path some fifty years ago, I am thrown back upon an interior experience that I would describe as a state of longing. What was it like, what was its direction, what was its quality? What I find is an almost childlike wish to be loved, accepted, and embraced. Behind this longing I sense that what will embrace me is something holy and pure. I long for that embrace, even while aware of my own impurities and imperfections. My longing is to be embraced and to become like that which embraces me. It is, essentially, a wish to completely enter into a quality of purity and holiness myself through being embraced by that purity and holiness.

I also recognize the yearning to know a God that is just and will bring justice and mercy to a troubled world, restoring the rights that have been violated, protecting the innocent that suffer so terribly. Yet both these longings are in reality one longing. It is a longing for the kingdom of God, in the language of Jesus.

Rumi has another analogy to describe our situation. The human being is like a reed that has been cut from the reed bed and has become a flute. We, as hollow reeds, never stop longing to return to our Source, the original reed bed. And as the great sacred traditions agree, the Divine has breathed its Spirit into us, and . . .

> This flute is played with fire, not with breath,
> and without this fire you would not exist.
> It is the fire of love that inspires the flute.
> It is the ferment of love that completes the wine.
>
> Pressed to the lips of one in harmony with myself,
> I might also tell all that can be told;
> but without a common tongue, I am dumb,

even if I have a hundred songs to sing.
When the rose is gone and the garden faded
You will no longer hear the nightingale's song.

The Beloved is all; the lover just a veil.
The Beloved is living;
the lover is without a life of its own.

Mathnawi I, opening lines

The Archetype of the Lover

In the Sufi tradition, the word *lover* is used to describe the seeker. The lover is someone quite different from the nominal believer. For the nominal believer, the Divine is something to refer to in times of need, in the great passages of life—birth, marriage, death—but the lover longs to be continually in the presence of Divine Love.

Sufis are lovers. They love life, they love the creation, and most of all they love God. But they love God not as an object, a separate Divine Person, but as a unified field of oneness. Today, for many reasons, humanity is more capable than ever of understanding what lovers have known for so long: God is the love and intelligence underlying existence, the unity of the multiplicity through love. This is a magnificent truth with awesome implications for every aspect of life.

The ritual prayer is five times daily,
but the guide for lovers is the verse,
they who are in prayer continually.

Surah al-Marij 70:23

The headache of intoxication in those heads
isn't relieved by five times,
nor by five hundred thousand.
"Visit once a week" is not the ration for lovers;
the soul of sincere lovers has an intense craving to drink.

"Visit once a week" is not the ration for those fish,
since they feel no spiritual joy without the Sea.

Mathnawi VI, 2669–70

Lovers have a very direct relationship with the Divine. For them, the Divine is the ultimate beauty. They are more passionate about this than a teenager in the first throes of infatuation.

The sickness of love is not like any other;
Love is the astrolabe of God's mysteries.
Whether love is from heaven or earth,
it points to God.
However I may try to explain it,
when faced with Love Itself
I'm ashamed of my explanations.
Whatever the tongue can make clear,
Love's silence is better.
And though the pen wanted badly to write,
when it came to Love, its nib split apart.
When it was the turn of the intellect
to unfold the meaning of Love,
it stumbled like a donkey in the mud.
In the end, only Love
could explain Itself
and what it is to be a lover.

Mathnawi I, 110–11

The opening to love is accomplished through the heart, which is a cognitive instrument. In other words, it is through the heart that we glimpse the Real by means of the light of love.

Educating the Heart

Because we are living within a unified, conscious Reality, with its own will, intelligence, conscious purpose, and love, everything is a sign to be read by the heart, revealing the meanings and purpose of this Reality.

In the history of human aspiration, there are traditions of enlightenment, sacred texts, and sources of true knowledge that can guide us. Some of these sources count as objective revelations from the Absolute Intelligence. If we are sincere, over time we will be shown the truth of these revelations "in ourselves and on the farthest horizon" (*Surah Fuṣṣilat* 41:53). But if our hearts are diseased and hardened, if we are without humility, we cannot grasp the revelations that Reality offers.

What are the characteristics of those who have verified these revelations? They are patient. They are humble. They are generous. They are forgiving. They are loving. They are strong. They have established within themselves the Mysterion that allows these qualities to shine forth naturally and spontaneously. They have seen that these qualities are attributes of their own essence.

The most central question in human life is how to awaken and purify the heart. It is the organ of perception that puts us in touch with a qualitative reality. The heart perceives meaning and significance; it senses relationships; it reveals to us the significance of existing as a spiritual being in this infinite universe.

> The peerless God has made
> all the six directions a theater
> for the display of signs to the clear-seeing,
> so that, whatever animal or plant they look upon,
> they may feed on the meadows of Divine Beauty.
> And so God said to the mystic companions,
> "Wherever you turn, there is the face of God."
> (*Surah al-Baqarah* 2:115)
>
> *Mathnawi* VI, 3640

Our daughter has been riding horses since she was four years old, and now she is a trainer of horses. Her sensitivity to horses, her understanding of their ways, has taught me so much about the intelligence and emotions of horses. It's her love of horses that has enabled her to know their moods, their fears, their joys, and how to bring out the best in them. When she is among horses she has a qualitative perception that is enlivened far beyond what human beings generally have for each other.

We have all experienced that at certain times the heart is open, while at other times it is closed, insensitive, contracted. When we can awaken and purify the heart, we can come into direct contact with higher Reality and have the kind of experience that brings unity to the self, orders the inner life, and reshapes the personality.

The great beings—Buddha, Jesus, and Muhammad among them—did not come to propose dogmas or establish a religious hierarchy but to show a way by which human beings could awaken and purify their hearts. These great teachers demonstrated how we might come to rely upon the authentic, free, and independent knowing of the heart. These prophets and enlightened beings issued a call to simplicity and true sanity, guided by a spiritual minimalism that teaches us to rely upon what we innately have within ourselves that can connect us to Reality.

> Listen, open a window to God
> and begin to delight yourself
> by gazing upon Him through the opening.
> The business of love is to make that window in the heart,
> for the breast is illumined by the beauty of the Beloved.
> Gaze incessantly on the face of the Beloved!
> Listen, this is in your power, my friend!
>
> *Mathnawi* VI, 3095–97

The lover says, "My religion is to be kept alive by love." The mystic Muhyiddin ibn al-Arabi expressed how his heart was opened to countless expressions of the Divine through discovering the religion of love:

O Marvel! A garden within the flames.
My heart has become capable of every form:
it is a pasture for gazelles and a monastery for monks,
it is a temple for idols and the pilgrim's Kaaba,
the tables of the Torah and the book of the Qur'an.
I follow the religion of love:
whatever way love's camels take,
that is my religion and my faith.

The whole enterprise of spirituality is to consciously awaken to the ultimate principle of value, Divine Being, and thereby to transform the forces of our character into something both beautiful and useful. The heart is essential to this task.

If a wealthy person brings a hundred sacks of gold,
God will only say,
"Bring the heart, you who are bent double.
If the heart is pleased with you, I am pleased;
and if the heart is opposed to you, I am opposed.
I don't pay attention to 'you'; I look to the heart:
bring it, poor soul, as a gift to My door!
Its relation to you is also Mine."
"Paradise is at the feet of mothers." [hadith]
The heart is the mother and father
and origin of all creatures:
the one who knows the heart from the flesh is blessed.
You will say, "Look, I have brought a heart to You."
God will respond, "The world is full of these hearts.
Bring the heart that is the axis of the world
and the Soul of the soul of the soul of Adam."
The Ruler of all hearts is waiting
for a heart filled with light and goodness.

Mathnawi V, 881–88

"The heart is the axis of the world" and love's journey is the journey of every human being through all the levels of being. There is no journey more real, more true, more important. On this journey of love, we encounter many beauties, many loves, many lovable people, but eventually, beyond all these objects of love, we may be able *to be in love with Love, to know the Source of Love Itself.*

In such a state, it is possible to know there is no greater love than what Rumi called "love with no object," for then you have become Love Itself.

9

Conditions for the Sufi Process

THE HIGHER FORMS OF LOVE we spoke about in the previous chapter are not likely to be attained through reading or even through meditative practice alone. That love can be made possible through the knowledge applied in the laboratory of community, with mature companionship and mentoring, and with the *baraka*[1] of a living tradition.

People may be attracted to Sufism after witnessing Sema,[2] or experiencing zikr, or listening to Sufi music. They may catch the fragrance of ecstasy that is so lacking in worldly, secular life. Ecstasy is an innate yearning and right for every human being, which, if not acknowledged and honored, will be overtaken by addictive and compulsive behavior or by a self-numbing that is a kind of soul death.

The soul longs for ecstasy just as it longs for heaven, but if the soul is to attain a healthy ecstasy, it must attain sobriety as well. There are two kinds of sobriety: one that precedes ecstasy, and another, more mature sobriety that is capable of containing ecstasy and intoxication—a sobriety that surpasses drunkenness.

Authentic ecstasy, in our understanding, is not a self-indulgent intoxication but the discovery of the true dimensions of Being. To be worthy of such ecstasy, the soul must be purified of self-indulgent tendencies and develop a sober maturity capable of containing its ecstasy. This spiritual maturity is developed through a spirituality grounded in relationship.

A Relational Spirituality

Sufism is a relational spirituality, not a path for solitaries, hermits, recluses—at least not all the time. In Sufism, the individual's spiritual practice is nurtured and balanced within a pattern of relationships.

The energies and insights of spiritual practice find their application in relationships. A Sufi community is a context for developing not only higher consciousness but character as well. The ripened fruit of spiritual practice is beautiful character (*akhlaq*).

It would be a serious mistake to demand of the Sufi process what it was never meant to give: self-gratification, entertainment, and the satisfaction of unmet emotional needs, including the need for attention.

In the end, success does not just depend on the individual. It depends as well on a conscious grouping of people so as to amplify their capacities, as if a dozen lamps are brought together and a more ample light is generated. Mysteriously, each individual lamp seems to increase in brightness.

There can be no real spiritual attainment that is not reflected in the beauty of our relationships. Beginning with the relationships within our immediate spiritual family and eventually extending to our relationship with all of life, the quality of our relationships is the real test of spiritual maturity.

In fact, there is a danger that spiritual practices alone, if they are not balanced with and complemented by healthy, loving relationships, may lead to negative results. To name just a few of those negative results when community and friendship are neglected: the arrogance of feeling spiritually superior; obsessive-compulsive behaviors mistaken for spiritual discipline; excessive "witnessing" of experience that results in a dissociated state; and, of course "spiritual bypass," or using spirituality to avoid confronting our own unconscious psychological issues.

What a Sufi teacher is hoping to see in someone starting this spiritual journey is, first of all, sincerity. Spiritual sincerity is when we act for the sake of God alone—for instance, service without any expectation of reward. We hope to see a capacity for commitment, a sufficient intention to make this work a high priority in one's life. Finally, there is no more hopeful sign in an aspiring seeker than devotion—putting one's heart into the work itself. Then, perhaps, there may be the possibility of following the invisible current that returns us to our origin.

Relationship as Remembrance

Relationship as remembrance is the practice of making our relationships conscious and sacred by not falling into habitual patterns of self-centeredness. It means not falling asleep when we are with one another. Relationship as remembrance means sustaining presence and openness to one another.

How quickly we lose awareness of ourselves as soon as we enter into conversation with other people! How easily the superficial personality can take over when we are no longer engaged in specifically spiritual practices. How difficult it is at first to maintain presence in a conversation when the machine of personality takes over.

It may be possible to feel uplifted and spiritually content on a prayer carpet, but our individual practice is obviously imperfect if the shadows of egoism appear as soon as we enter into conversation or interaction with others.

We sometimes witness how people can go deep into a meditation or zikr, and shortly after—for instance, when tea is served—unconsciously resume their social personalities and waste in chitchat the fine energy that had been generated.

In the sacred space of a more traditional Sufi lodge, there would be little opportunity for such social banter. The rules would be strict and clearly defined. The decorum would not be violated. The dervishes would not only be silent in the presence of their shaikh but they would not so much as turn their backs to the shaikh.

Instituting the strict adab (manners; spiritual courtesy) of the traditional *dergah* (Sufi lodge) would seem very artificial in our contemporary world. On the other hand, in our more relaxed Sufi circles in the West, people have the opportunity to forget themselves, but the hope is that they will gradually learn to be present even in casual social interactions. Sometimes we have to be willing to risk living on the edge of adab in order to develop the mature capacity to carry presence into everyday life.

Relationship is where we are most often asleep when we most need to be awake. It is in relationship that we must overcome the artifice of the false self that obstructs true connection with each other.

Sophisticated, educated people prize and even fortify their individuality, but they may be quite undeveloped in their capacities for relationship. We may not realize how much our own suffering derives from the pretense of individuality. The false self is mostly built upon vanity and pride, or its opposites, low self-esteem and shame. And it is these factors that impede genuine relationship. Some people are overidentified with their ethnicity or ancestry, with their education or looks. Others carry the burden of low self-esteem or let themselves be defined by their emotional wounds.

Relationship deepens as we unite in our common interests as human beings, realizing in humility that we are more alike than unlike each other. Mevlana Jalaluddin Rumi says that if you want to know love, become "We." It is the sacred We that is the real crucible of transformation. Relationship deepens as we bracket our sense of separateness and honor our common purpose. True individuality will not be lost; it will be developed in relationship with others.

Relationships of expedience, heedlessness, callousness, and exploitation are the ways of the world. Relationships of goodwill, loyalty, and love reflect the truth and harmony of higher worlds.

If you speak well of another, the good will return to you. The good and praise you speak of another you speak in reality of yourself. A parallel would be when someone plants a garden and herb bed around his house. Every time he looks out, he sees flowers and herbs. If you accustom yourself to speak well of others, you are always in a "paradise." When you do a good deed for someone else, you become a friend to him, and whenever he thinks of you he will think of you as a friend—and thinking of a friend is as restful as a flower garden. When you speak ill of someone else, you become detestable in his sight so that whenever he thinks of you he will imagine a snake or a scorpion, or thorns and thistles. Now, if you can look at the flowers in a garden day and night, why would you wander in a briar patch or a snake pit? Love everybody so that you may always stay among the flowers of the garden. If you hate everybody and imagine enemies everywhere, it would be like wandering day and night in a briar patch or snake pit.

The saints love everybody and see everything as good, not for anyone else's sake but for their own, lest a hateful, detestable image come into their view. Since there is no choice in this world but to think of people, the saints have striven to think of everybody as a friend so that hatred may not mar their way.

So, everything you do with regard to people and every mention you make of them, good or evil, will all return to you. Hence God says, "He who does right, does it to the advantage of his own soul; and he who does evil, does it against the same" (*Surah Fuṣṣilat* 41:46) and "Whoever shall have wrought evil of the weight of an ant, shall behold the same" (*az-Zalzalah* 99:8).

Signs of the Unseen [Fihi ma fihi], Discourse 15

Relationship becomes the mirror in which we see ourselves more clearly. In the end, relationship is the mosque in which we must learn to prostrate and surrender the false self.

Adab and Conscious Relationship

Some years ago, a group of American representatives of traditional Sufi lineages were informally gathered in San Francisco. Someone proposed a question: Of all that this tradition has taught us, what stands out as most important and valuable?

Now, Sufism is a path comprising not only personal practice but a way of life and vast culture. We were, moreover, all trained in different orders and from cultures as diverse as Turkey, North Africa, Iran, and South Asia. I think we were all startled by how quickly we arrived at a consensus that adab stood out as the most uniquely valuable teaching we had received.

Neither our American culture nor the times we lived in had put much emphasis on "manners." We had been a rough-and-tumble generation that passed through a period of rebellion toward what we saw as the hypocrisies of our society. Informality was viewed as real and authentic behavior; manners, or etiquette, would have been, at best, a quaint and irrelevant concept. What, then, would account for the magnetic power of adab?

From what I remember of our conversation that day, we seemed to think that adab had enabled a certain quality of relationship among ourselves, across the boundaries of our orders, and in the teaching situation within our own communities. It had softened our egos and introduced a quality of refinement in our relationships. On the path of Sufism, my own idea of spiritual attainment had been transformed from a notion of some austere and impersonal enlightenment to an embodied humility. This is not to say that any of us felt we had attained this ideal, but we held an image of it in our hearts, an image that had been formed by contact with certain of our teachers who were, for the most part, examples of humility, sincerity, sensitivity, respect, and courtesy—in short, adab.

Some of the best examples of adab are those I have seen being lived in some Sufi families. For example, we have known and welcomed as guests into our home three generations of the direct descendants of Jalaluddin Rumi. A more cultivated and courteous family I have never known. Adab is reflected in every aspect of life: dressing, eating, serving food, speaking, welcoming guests. I remember one cold winter morning in our farmhouse in Vermont when I came down to the "mudroom" (you have to have lived in a place like rural Vermont to truly appreciate what a mudroom is for) to find that the dozens of shoes and winter boots had all been aligned in rows with the toes pointing into the house. Jelal Chelebi, the twenty-year-old, twenty-third-generation descendant of Rumi, had taken it upon himself to put our shoes in order. Instantly it came back to me that in Turkey I had never seen a chaos of shoes in a Sufi home, and I remembered: this is our adab. I had forgotten. Yet when I thanked our young Chelebi, it was clear that this ordering that he had taken on himself was not an expression of a "should" as much as an act of humble service.

I have observed that children in Sufi families are lovingly given subtle cues about how to act and move through the world. Abdulbaki Golpinarli, perhaps the greatest documenter of Turkish Sufi life in the last century, wrote about his own upbringing in this way:

> I remember that, when I was a child, if I walked quickly, or stamped my feet, people would say to me (not out of anger), "What are you doing, Baki? What kind of a way is that to walk? My child, everything has a heart, a life, a soul; wouldn't the wood get hurt? Look, it's laid itself on the floor for us to walk on. Shouldn't we show respect, and not hurt it?"
>
> If I smacked my lips during a meal, all it took to stop me was a look. Except for conversation, a meal was to be silent. If one made a noise by setting one's glass down, for instance, it was considered unmannerly, a sort of minor sin; neither the glass nor the place one put it on should be treated carelessly. What a bad thing it was to drink water without interacting with the glass, without kissing it before drinking from it, or again before putting it back down! "The glass," they would say, "is serving us; we should honor it." While going to sleep every night and again while waking up every morning, I would kiss the pillow; while pulling the sheets up over me or taking them off, I would interact with them as well.[3]

In the Mevlevi tradition, this respect was extended to inanimate objects to such an extent that one would never, for instance, say, "Please put out the candle" but rather "Put the candle to rest." Nor would one "close" a door but "cover" it. Fastidious care was taken to convey in language a positive respect. And for every object that one uses in daily life, one would engage in a reciprocal seeing with the object. In other words, as I pick up my coat, I might kiss it lightly, see it, and *be seen by it*. In Turkish there is a phrase that literally means "seeing with it." Golpinarli continues,

> In our household, we wouldn't shout to each other or interrupt someone while he was speaking; and when in a group, we would speak to the whole group, not just to one or two people. The idea of whispering in someone's ear or of laughing loudly was foreign to our household.[4]

The practical outcome of adab is to help create an atmosphere of sharing, unity, coherence. I have come to expect that within a Sufi environment, conversation around a table does not quickly break up into several personal discussions with whomever is adjacent but proceeds as a shared experience at the table. If one had reason to address another person, one wouldn't thereby cut oneself off from the conversation of the whole.

Another aspect of adab is being conscious when one uses the words *I* or *me*, if one uses them at all. In certain Sufi orders, for instance, it would be customary not to use the word *I* at all while working or serving in the *tekkye* (Sufi lodge). Some prefer to refer to themselves as "this fakir," meaning someone who is destitute and utterly dependent on God for everything.

How different is this milieu of social interaction from the one we so commonly experience in our society. How often do we find ourselves in situations where conversation may be dominated unconsciously by whomever is a good talker or whomever commands and holds the attention of others, whether or not the rest of the people at the table are particularly interested. In the adab of learning, one may need to cultivate listening and receptivity and even control one's urge to immediately express one's own opinion.

It isn't easy to convey this way of being to people of the modern world. To become critical and judgmental because others may fail in their adab would be rude and antithetical to adab itself. And for adab to degenerate into rigid formality would also belie its essence, for there is a proper adab for every situation. Among intimate friends, for example, the proper adab may sometimes be utter informality and ease. Adab is best learned by example and in community, and once we have some grasp of its potential, it might begin to play more of a role in our own lives, schools, and organizations.

It is said that there is an adab within spiritual circles, with parents and children, with elders, and even with God. Al Hujwiri, an early (d. 1077) commentator on Sufism, wrote,

> A person who neglects this discipline cannot ever possibly be a saint, for the Prophet said, "*Adab* is a mark of those whom God loves." One must keep oneself from disrespect toward God in one's private as well as one's public behavior. We have it from a sound hadith that once, when God's Messenger was sitting with his legs akimbo, the Angel Gabriel appeared and said, "Muhammad, sit as servants sit before a master."[5]

There is a story of a Sufi, Muhasibi, who for forty years never stretched out his legs even when alone (to point the soles of one's feet directly in the direction of others is not considered well-mannered in many cultures outside of America). When questioned, he answered, "I am ashamed to sit otherwise than as a servant while I remember God."

It should be emphasized, however, that in Sufi understanding, substance takes precedence over form; inner intention counts for more than outer behavior. The Prophet Muhammad, peace and blessings upon him, said that the ritual prayer must be accompanied by presence (*hudhur*) to be valid, so it is not the outer form itself that is obligatory. And at the same time, Rumi proposes that the observance of these outer requirements are gifts testifying to Love. Properly understood and consciously applied, attention to the details of form is a way of working on our own essence. Ritual prayer gives the body an experience of surrender that would be difficult to achieve in any other way.

The Prophet Muhammad is known to have acted in specific ways—always putting on the right sandal first, or stepping into a house with the right foot and out of it with the left. His behavior is widely imitated. Some formalists insist on imitating his behavior as if there was something objectively better about using the right foot first. Could it be that these behaviors might be reminders to help us live more consciously?

The outer aspect of adab is intended to guide us toward greater consciousness and to inner sincerity. The form is not an end in itself but a potential container for qualities of being such as sincerity, reverence, presence, and love.

Our perspective is continually informed by an awareness of levels of reality, inner purification, qualities of consciousness. Four levels of attainment are commonly described:

Shari'ah, the level of religious law and external morals. In the Qur'an, where shari'ah is mentioned only once, it describes the broad path to human well-being: a healthy, balanced, and moral human life. What is typically referred to as the "shari'ah" today is a collection of legal and ethical formulations of scholars beginning in the second century of Islam. Unfortunately, in some people's minds it degenerates into a self-righteous legalism and various forms of authoritarian behavior. We would do well to keep in mind Muhammad's injunction: Woe to anyone who makes this religion (or path) difficult for others.

Tariqah, the esoteric path. At its best, tariqah is a complete education of the human being under the guidance of a teacher—that is, with the friendship of someone more advanced on the Way. At its worst, it may sometimes degenerate into cultish and even superstitious behavior, although such distortions have been relatively un-common given the lived example of the Prophet Muhammad, which was utterly humble, grounded, and practical.

Marifah, gnosis or realization; the goal to which the path should lead. On the spiritual path, the self becomes free not by breaking through the bounds of the sacred law but by discovering the source of the law within the depths of the heart. This is made possible through the objective experience of a purified consciousness.

Haqiqah, realization of Truth, apprehension of the Real, inti-macy with the Divine, and the corresponding transformation of character that this brings about.

Among the Sufis, adab practically became their shari`ah. Instead of merely avoiding immoral and destructive behavior, the Sufis at-tempted to embody the qualities of kindness, thoughtfulness, gener-osity, and self-sacrifice.

Now, with these distinctions in mind, here is a story as told by Abdulbaki Golpinarli that shows how he as a young child was taught the significance of adab in relationship to the mystical path:

One day, I went to a *tekkye* with Ahmed Hamdi Tanyeli to ask a question. I knocked on the door of the harem, and we heard a shrill female voice, as if it was scolding us: "Who is it?"

Ahmed Hamdi Tanyeli said that it must be the tenants. We asked for the shaikh.

The woman shrieked again: "They are on the other side of the building."

"I told you so," said Ahmed Hamdi.

We went to the *selamlik*, the part of the building reserved for greeting people outside the immediate family. From the main entrance we walked through the garden and knocked on the door. From inside we heard a sweet voice ask us, "Who is it?" We asked for the shaikh.

She replied, "He has traveled to Allah." We asked for his son. The sweet voice said, "He has gone as well." She asked if we needed anything. "Please, sit on the bench in the garden," she said, "and this fakir will soon come to you."

We sat down. After a couple of minutes, a middle-aged woman came out and served us cups of Turkish coffee. She sat down and greeted us. We told her what we had come for, and she gave us as much information as she could.

We talked a little more, and then we asked for permission to leave. She accompanied us to the door, and as we departed we heard behind us her sweet voice saying, "Goodbye! Be well! You brought good luck. *Inshallah*, come back again."

Ahmed Tanyeli turned to me and said, "That first place we went to was shari`ah;[6] this place is tariqah."[7]

It will certainly seem unfair in the eyes of some to dismiss or even condemn the level of shari`ah in this way. One cannot deny that the fundamental ethics of outer behavior are essential to justice and social well-being, and that shari`ah itself teaches a basic adab. Perhaps what the shaikh was pointing to is the need for another level of awareness. Sufis refer to an "adab of service": the realization that every moment of our lives can be lived in service to Allah. If such an adab were to permeate one's life, one would know how little belongs to us and how much is owed to God.

For many years I have reflected on how this word, *adab*, can be translated. "Etiquette," "manners," "decorum," "thoughtfulness"—no single word adequately captures it, which is why we continue to use the word *adab* even in English. Interestingly, the term for the faculty of literature in a university is called *adabiyyah*, which suggests refinement and culture. To have adab is to be cultured.

It has been said that the highest attainment of Sufism is nothing but good character. What is meant, however, is not a moralistic personality commanded by external expectations but a natural, spontaneous beauty of character that is the result of a long maturing process of transformation. Adab is the ability to sense what is appropriate to each moment and to give to each its due—a continuous process of refining one's speech and actions. The ripened fruit of this kind of understanding and practice is not an abstract and impersonal enlightened person but a person of extraordinariness with whom you would love to sit down and have a cup of tea. It is an embodied spirituality.

Establishing Presence

The foundation of adab is presence, that state of awareness that stands above thought, emotion, behavior, and sense perception but that comprehends them all. With presence we are fully conscious that we are alive, that we *are*. With presence our experience of life becomes more spacious. With presence we become aware of a wider context for our life and we develop a capacity to freely direct our attention.

Presence is the bridge, the interworld, between our everyday identity and God. Actually, there are countless levels of experience between the solidified ego and God, and presence is the key to all of them. In other words, we can experience presence on increasingly subtle levels beginning with being present to our own physical bodies, then our emotions, then our thoughts, then our subtle intentions and emotional attitudes, all the way up to an experience of the Divine Presence Itself.

By bringing our full attention to the present moment and what we are doing, we open up a space that is relatively free of random, habitual thoughts. We assume some mastery over our own inner experience. We redirect our attention from the preoccupations of our habitual self. Instead of unconsciously seeking various forms of self-gratification (pleasure, comfort, the positive regard of others), we turn our attention to simply being in the present moment. Gradually this capacity to direct and refine our attention increases and we begin to experience that there is something quite whole and satisfying about this experience of Being itself.

Over time our sense of who we are can undergo a significant

transformation. Our sense of self acquires a new spaciousness, peace, and stability. Whereas we used to experience ourselves as our thoughts and emotions, much of it quite negative in character, now we begin to have an experience of ourselves as something beyond thought, feeling, sense perception, and behavior. It is not that we do not experience various desires, responses, and negative states but that these do not entirely extinguish and replace the sense of our own abiding presence.

If we continue to practice, there may also be more dramatic experiences—moments of grace and realization, intimacy with God, wonder and awe.

On the Sufi path, presence is consistently developed through the primary practices of *salaat* (the ritual prayer) and zikr (remembrance through the Names, whether aloud or in silence). The ritual prayer awakens presence in movement and action, and, more importantly, leads us to an embodied experience of surrender to the Infinite. It is a fundamentally grounding practice. Zikr, on the other hand, attunes us in a more inward way. With zikr we spiral into the dimensionless point within our own being, where we are closest to God.

Spiritual practice is also a context in which we develop sincerity. We learn to put aside the incessant demands of the ego and remember our heart's yearning. It is easy to fool ourselves on the spiritual path by claiming that we want spiritual development and freedom from our own selfish egos while living our lives in an unconscious slavery to the ego.

The ego will even critique our spiritual path and practice in all sorts of ways: raising doubts, inventing excuses, and justifying our own laziness. The ego may even propose that everyday life, in and of itself, is our spiritual practice. While there is some truth in this proposition, there is also room for self-deception in it. Some will say they live in a state of worship and so specific times and forms of worship are unnecessary. But would anyone be foolish enough to say that since I can snack whenever I like, therefore I will forgo breakfast, lunch, and dinner? We need those spiritual mealtimes to be able to sustain ourselves between meals, so to speak.

While it may be true that at a high level of attainment, enlightenment is everyday life and everyday life is enlightenment, we need to find a practical way of attaining this realization and sustaining it. All of life is movement, but not all movement is exercise. An intelligent, concentrated form of movement can develop muscle tone in a way that ordinary movement cannot. So, too, spiritual practice is a concentrated exercise of the soul that helps us to keep our soul fit for the challenges of life.

In Sufism, spiritual practice can be distilled to the following areas of practice:

ORIENTATION	CAPACITY TO DEVELOP	FOCUS OF THE WORK	POSITIVE IDEAL
Coming into presence, self-awareness	Conscious breath	Embracing the moment	spontaneity, *ibn al waqt*
Awakening intention	Reason	Overcoming distraction	sincerity, intention, *himma*
Sustaining awareness	Attention	Inner talking	equanimity, openness, *tawakkul*
Transcending self-interest	Sensing	Lies & traps of the false self	humility, modesty, *fana*
Opening to remembrance	Stillness	Heedlessness	love of God, faith, *ashq*

Orientation	Capacity to Develop	Focus of the Work	Positive Ideal
Expressing gratitude & awe	Voice	Overcoming fear, presumption	wonder, creativity, *baqa*
Radiating blessing	Love	Withdrawing from fantasy & negativity	generosity, purity, *rahmah*

Making Worship the Rhythm of Life

Of all human activities, worship—provided it is with presence—is the most direct route to contact with the Infinite.

Worship in communion with sincere seekers and lovers of God is even more fruitful than worship alone. Worship that includes the whole of us is vastly more effective than worship that only includes a part of us. Worship can begin in stillness of mind, heart, and body, leading to an inner activation, a deep recollection in which we make a spontaneous and specific call to Spirit, asking of it all the qualities and strengths we need to serve in life. This spontaneous prayer (*du'a*) can be clear and resonant, since through the voice it is possible to awaken the dormant essence within ourselves and others.

What is prayer? It is the outpouring of the soul to the Source of Soul. Worship is sustained by a sense of relationship with a higher power, a source of help and guidance. In worship we stand in humility and awe of that power, we experience repentance and regret for our heedlessness, and we hope for mercy and forgiveness.

Truly, my prayer, my sacrifice, my life and my death are for God, the Sustainer of the Universes.

Surah al-An'am 6:163

86

Why is worship necessary? What makes us human is the vast capacity of our soul. Without this soul—this spiritual dimension of consciousness, will, reason, and love—the human is only an animal.

Worship is the food of the soul. Without worship, the soul is undernourished, starved of the spiritual nourishment. If the soul is not strong, the animal and egotistical side of our nature gains the upper hand, leading to dispersion, dissatisfaction, and ultimately estrangement from Being. On the other hand, with continual worship, the soul is strengthened through friendship with the Source of Soul.

Sustainer, make us submissive to You, and make out of our offspring a people submissive to You, and show us Your ways of worship, and accept our repentance: surely You alone are the Acceptor of Repentance, the Infinitely Compassionate.

Surah al-Baqarah 2:128

This is the continual prayer of the faithful human being, a recognition of our human imperfections, and a drawing near to the Source of Infinite Compassion. And the following verses instruct the faithful to turn to a genuine source of sustenance:

Therefore, bear with patience whatever they say, and extol the limitless glory of your Sustainer, and praise Him, before the rising of the sun and before its setting, and glorify Him for some of the night and some of the day, so that you might attain tranquility. And do not turn your eyes toward that which We have allowed others to enjoy during the pleasing time of this world's life, so that they might be tested by it, for the sustenance that your Sustainer provides is better and more enduring. And encourage your people to pray, and be persevering yourself. We don't expect you to provide; for it is We who provide the sustenance for you. And the ultimate outcome is God-consciousness.

Surah Ṭa Ha 20:130–32

Worship is real when we can sense the beauty, the "glory" of the Source of Being and are not distracted by the shallow attractions of the surface reality.

When it is said "There are no gods but God," it implies that we shall worship only what is truly Divine, that we shall recognize the Beneficent Reality behind the forms and events of our lives. Idolatry, in any form, is the fundamental sin, that which separates us from the Real. When we make an idol of the self, we increase self-will, self-justification, self-righteousness, and self-indulgence.

The common idolatries of the contemporary world include busyness, inordinate ambition, the compulsive need for intoxication and entertainment, misplaced sexual desire, and the need to attract the attention of others.

Whatever commands our attention is our master. Whatever we worship consciously or unconsciously is what we serve. If we serve the Ultimate Source, we are freed from thousands of other masters.

> The ultimate purpose of this world
> is nothing but worship.
> Though the final object of a book
> is the knowledge that it contains,
> you can also make it a pillow to rest upon;
> it will serve as that, too.
> But it was not created to be used as a pillow.
> It was really intended for learning and knowledge
> and the benefit that comes from these.
>
> *Mathnawi* III, 2989–90

If we value something more than Spirit, it is because of a misapprehension, a narrowness of vision. If we are identified with our small, partial self, we will be captured in the net of desires. If we are in an intimate relationship with Spirit, what we desire will be the desire of wholeness.

If you wish for the light, prepare yourself
to receive it; if you wish to be far from God,
nourish your egoism and drive yourself away.
If you wish to find a way out of this ruined prison,
don't turn your head away from the Beloved
but bow in worship and draw near.

Mathnawi I, 3605–7

The soul has the natural tendency to soar higher and higher since it originally came from the Most High. We are not bound only to this worldly level, whatever its attractions may be. It is through worship that the veil between earth and heaven is lifted.

10

The Sense of the Sacred

Restoring Wisdom-Based Intelligence

What occupies most people in the contemporary world most of the time is a superficial search for love, pleasure, and security. We live in a culture dominated by these outer concerns to such an extent that the search for spiritual meaning, if it is acknowledged at all, is most often acknowledged for its absence.

Knowledge has come to mean mere analytical and quantitative reasoning, a manipulative cunning, extroverted and often heartless.

To the extent that anyone searches for knowledge, it is not the knowledge of the sacred but rather a knowledge of external things and the means to effect change in the material or social world. Even most of the available self-help books are aimed at developing a self that is more efficient in attaining its desires: work less, earn more; make yourself indispensable; attract prosperity.

The intentional cultivation of inner spiritual experience is an arcane, forgotten discipline. The appreciation and mastery of that quality of human experience that might truly be called spiritual is something we may read about in books but rarely come across in everyday life.

The experience of the sacred is not a continual presence in most people's lives. Instead, it is a rather rare experience to be discovered, perhaps, in moments alone in nature, or in those times when everything that we normally occupy ourselves with has been completely overturned by crisis or catastrophe. We turn in this direction, finally, when we have run out of all other options.

And if the surrounding culture is almost entirely preoccupied with trivial pursuits, dominated by worries and fears whether real or imaginary, and caught up in the glitter of technology and the mostly purposeless rush of consumption, our own souls are inevitably affected.

Our innate intelligence is reduced to a mere problem-solving, strategizing faculty or, worse yet, we live in a state of continual reaction. Our very selfhood, occupied and distracted with outer concerns, becomes contracted. The hard shell of egoism thickens; governed by thoughts and emotions associated with these outer, superficial, and negative preoccupations, our life passes until eventually it reaches its end.

Those who walk the streets and drive the highways of the contemporary world would hardly imagine that knowledge was once a means to bliss or that intelligence could seek out the fragrance of the sacred.

Yet to understand the nature and purpose of our human intelligence is vitally important to our souls. Our intelligence is not merely something of practical, utilitarian value in the world but, insofar as it can bring us an immediate experience of Truth, it opens us to dimensions of beauty, happiness, illumination, and love. Spiritual intelligence is the means by which our souls are perfected.

The wisdom dimension of intelligence has largely been abandoned for the exploitive and mechanical aspects of mere thought. But the highest intelligence is essentially a ray of the Divine Light reflected in the human being, which can lead us to discover a deeper reality, both on the farthest horizons of the outer worlds and within ourselves.

Even the rationale for a wisdom-based intelligence has been lost and replaced by methods of measurement and heartless analysis. The natural theology that saw the human being in the context of a spiritual reality, that saw human intelligence as a reflection of Divine Intelligence, has been discredited by a mentality that regards reality as what presents itself to the senses for measurement.

There is an urgent need today to imagine a community whose mission and intention is to awaken and develop a wisdom-based intelligence, both individually and collectively. Spiritual intelligence cannot awaken solely as an individual process; the individual's awakening is dependent to some extent on the relationships and synergy within a community that shares common principles. Eventually, of course, this awakened intelligence must and will have its effect within societies and the larger human community, but it begins with conscious individuals in small communities where a subculture of wisdom might flourish. It is not an exaggeration to say that the safeguarding of our humanness depends on the establishment of such communities.

Societies in Collapse

Because there are not enough individuals with this awakened spiritual intelligence in our technocratic societies, the most basic principles of perennial wisdom are being disregarded. By reducing all of life to the material—in other words, to whatever can be quantified through the senses—today's societies disregard the sacred in human relationships, nature, economic transactions, medicine, and, in fact, every discipline of human life.

This is the reason why everything around us is collapsing. We cannot help but notice how much in the modern world does not work. The absence and depletion of the sacred is not merely the loss of some nonessential transcendent quality. It leads to the accumulation of many negative practical and tangible effects. It could be said that the more a sense of the sacred is absent in individuals, the more we will face deteriorating conditions of human dignity and well-being:

Everyday life will be an experience of alienation.
People will be perceived as objects, as things, as other.
Mistrust and selfishness will increasingly contaminate human relationships.

93

Human intimacy will more and more disappear, or be replaced by "virtual" relationships, artificially mediated contacts.

Life will be understood through materialistic explanations.

People will seek happiness in external satisfactions.

The development of inner qualities and capacities will be disregarded.

Education will focus on operations, not values and principles.

Profits will be made without regard for human benefit.

Solutions to problems will focus more on symptoms, less on causes, especially when the causes are beyond the range of materialist explanations.

And all in all, the human soul will be diminished because it has not been valued.

Increasingly we will live in a world where:

Human settlements offer economic opportunity without community.

Food, the very basis of life, will become a product that doesn't nourish.

Art will become entertainment and mere spectacle.

Entertainment will numb and stupefy rather than reveal and inspire.

Medicine will not heal but will be a source of profit.

Armies will not guarantee peace but engender perpetual war.

Financial institutions will not protect wealth but centralize it.

Government will not protect freedoms but control through power and surveillance.

And all in all, the conditions for human dignity and self-realization will be in decline.

The sacred is both our origin and our purpose. As much as we lack an awareness of the sacred, we lack meaning, for the sacred is the highest truth of existence. What is sacred is something that has the fragrance or imprint of the Eternal.

Even the best of religions have today become mere shells of their true reality. To the extent that they focus on externals, religions have been hollowed out, their inner dimensions excavated and left on the garbage heap of the modern world. To the extent that the institutional leaders of major religions have participated in this devaluation, they have impoverished their religions. Those very religions are being rejected by the majority of humanity. People are walking away from meaningless, superficial beliefs and activities that offer little for the inner reality of human beings.

The Inheritance of Spiritual Intelligence

Yet despite the depletion of the wisdom dimension of intelligence in the contemporary world, every human being carries an inheritance of spiritual intelligence, which is the reflection of Universal Intellect on the human plane. The particular, individualized intellect of each human being is potentially a portal for the streaming of Universal Intellect, the awesome intelligence that we are meant to develop.

> Listen, open a window to God
> and begin to delight yourself
> by gazing upon Him through the opening.
> The business of love is to make that window in the heart,
> for the breast is illumined by the beauty of the Beloved.
> Gaze incessantly on the face of the Beloved!
> Listen, this is in your power, my friend!
>
> *Mathnawi* VI, 3095–97

In the Islamic understanding, this intelligence is a faculty implanted in Adam, who is "everyman," the archetypal human being.

Spiritual intelligence grants the ability to discern the absolute from the relative—in other words, to know the Divine within this physical existence. But it is we who must rediscover the fact that the purpose of our innate intelligence is to know reality adequately, objectively, totally.

> O Sea of Bliss, O You who have stored
> transcendental forms of consciousness in the heedless,
> You have stored a wakefulness in sleep;
> You have fastened dominion over the heart
> to the state of one who has lost his heart.
> You conceal riches in the lowliness of poverty;
> You fasten the necklace of wealth to poverty's iron collar.
> Opposite is secretly concealed in opposite:
> fire is hidden within boiling water.
> A delightful garden is hidden within Nimrod's fire:
> income multiplies from giving and spending—
> so that Muhammad, the king of prosperity, has said,
> "O possessors of wealth, generosity is a gainful trade."
> Riches were never diminished by almsgiving:
> in truth, acts of charity
> are an excellent means of increasing one's wealth.
>
> *Mathnawi* VI, 3567–73

We are equipped by our very nature to be able to know many levels of reality and to experience a state of well-being and peace by communing with a Presence that is always here, no matter what our outer circumstances are.

Our intelligence can know the Ultimate Reality as something that transcends all the outer circumstances of existence and, simultaneously, as something that is profoundly immanent within ourselves. The purpose of human intelligence, and therefore of human life, is to recognize that we are fundamentally rooted in the sacred.

If we can nurture a community of men and women committed to spiritual transformation, we will manifest Divine Blessing, *Baraka*.

Truly, in the creation of the heavens and the earth, and in the succession of night and day, there are indeed messages for all who are endowed with insight, and who remember God when they stand, and when they sit, and when they lie down to sleep, and thus reflect on the creations of the heavens and the earth: "O our Sustainer! You have not created any of this without meaning and purpose. *Limitless are You in Your Glory. Deliver us from the anguish of the Fire.*"

Surah al `Imran 3:190–91

11

The Queen of Intelligences

The Recognition of the Sacred in Life

Abu Hamid al-Ghazali, one of the foremost figures in medieval Islamic spirituality, once wrote, "Sufism is the best way to the highest truth." At the time that he made this statement, official representatives of Islamic civilization favored law and ethics more than contemplation and love. The world has changed in the nine centuries since al-Ghazali, but we can say that we now live in a civilization that favors science and business more than contemplation and love.

The discipline of Sufism is a comprehensive spiritual education that integrates every aspect of life through the power of spiritual intelligence. Spiritual intelligence is the queen of intelligences because it is that human faculty that is capable of recognizing and experiencing what is fundamentally true, good, and beautiful. It is therefore the most comprehensive intelligence, and all other forms of intelligence should ideally serve spiritual intelligence. Science, art, ethics, economics, and law all together reach a high expression and are harmonized when they are brought under the organizing principle of the highest truth.

Neither spiritual intelligence nor this highest truth is susceptible to precise formulation, definition, or conceptualization, although various traditions will offer their own vocabulary, metaphors, and ontological concepts. Spiritual intelligence resides in the human heart and that is where it must be developed and experienced.

From the personal perspective, this highest truth is approached when we ask ourselves what we truly value. Wherever the human being senses value—the value of life, beauty, meaning—there is something that might be recognized as *sacred*.

If we look beyond the exclusively religious meaning of this word, we find a more general definition: worthy of reverence and respect. Almost any human being, therefore, holds something sacred. This holds true even for those people who claim to believe in a totally materialistic reality, for no one can live as a human being without some sense of values. Ask anyone, "What do you hold sacred?" and it is almost certain that they will have an answer.

The experience and recognition of the sacred brings us beyond a merely quantitative and materialistic framework. It adds a qualitative dimension of intelligence, a dimension of meaning and values.

The Dimension of Meaning and Values

Spiritual intelligence doesn't negate or compete with other forms of intelligence, but it may qualify them, elevate them, and bring them into coherence.

Science, in and of itself, has no values other than scientific verification. As such it may be employed for any purpose, moral or immoral, life-enhancing or life-destroying. Scientific progress alone may easily lead to a dystopian future in which our essential human qualities are overwhelmed by technological marvels, shallow spectacle, synthetic sentiments, and merely transactional relationships. Insulated from the natural electromagnetic fields in which human life has evolved, now bathed in the frequencies of an internet of things, we may lose all sense of natural feeling and gradually adapt to the soullessness of a post-human, post-nature environment.

On the other hand, if science can cooperate with the spiritual awareness of human beings, through their subjective experience of states of coherence, focus, flow, and peace, science may be used to correct the dehumanizing imbalances, artificialities, and distortions that technologies themselves have caused.

Science and technology have not been applied in objective and impartial ways, but have sometimes been subservient to human egoism, greed, and aggression. Science and technology, for example, have often conceived themselves as being at war with nature, seeking to conquer and dominate nature rather than learn from it.

On the other hand, the developing field of biomimicry, in which science observes and learns from nature, is leading to technological innovations that can benefit human life and the environment. Nature is a superb designer, engineer, and healer.

It has been recently discovered, for instance, that certain fungi can reprocess the most toxic industrial pollutants and in a relatively short time transform them into life-supporting, nourishing substances.

The discovery of laws of proportion, and especially the mathematics of the vortex, have been used to engineer effective and energy-saving devices. And these are just the beginning of the discoveries that are possible if we take a more qualitative, more spiritual approach to research and development.

If science and technology can learn from nature's ways, they can avoid the dangers of a blind materialistic science inimical to human well-being. If science can be guided by spiritual intelligence, it can link itself with true human needs and be made more harmonious with human life.

Nature is just one level of manifestation. As science begins to comprehend the implications of nonlocal reality, quantum entanglement, scalar energies, nature, and human life have the possibilities of flourishing in a more coherent and beautiful understanding of the whole.

Likewise, economic or legal systems that ignore the dimension of values in human life will serve only greed and power. Capital will be unleashed serving its own purposes at the expense of human life and values.

Religion that is out of alignment with spiritual intelligence will concern itself merely with appearances rather than substance, with outer rituals and forms rather than substance and sincerity. Religion that only pays lip service to sacred values betrays the sacred and actually serves power and privilege.

And literature, music, and the arts may be reduced to merely neurotic expression, exhibitionism, and commercialism unless they somehow express something that touches the heart, something that expresses the spiritual nature of existence.

Is this the kind of world our children will inherit? What is left when the purpose and value of life is forgotten? Will a soulless technocracy prevail or will humanity rescue itself from its own creations? Since spiritual intelligence is concerned with the perception of absolute reality, it is concerned with absolute value.

Living Under the Light of the Eternal

Sufism is a way of life that aims to always remember the highest, most beautiful truth and to subject every aspect of life to a rigorous examination according to the highest values. Rumi, for instance, is continually shining his light upon ordinary human experience and illuminating it with his sublime spiritual intelligence. Consider how each of the following quatrains[1] opens us to a dimension of spiritual awareness.

> In comfort and abundance the Friend raised me.
> With vein and skin He tailored this ragged body.
> It's just a robe worn by a Sufi, the heart.
> The whole universe is a *khaneqah*[2] and He is my shaikh.
>
> Quatrain 33

> With the Beloved's life-giving waters,
> there is no disease,
> In the Beloved's garden of union,
> there are no thorns.
> They say between our hearts

there's a shutter we can open,
but what is there to open if no walls remain?

Quatrain 511

To us a different language has been given,
And a place besides heaven and hell.
Those whose hearts are free
have a different soul,
a pure jewel excavated from a different mine.

Quatrain 403

If you desire the self, get out of the self.
Leave the shallow stream behind
and flow into the river deep and wide.
Don't be an ox pulling the wheel of the plow,
turn with the stars that wheel above you.

Quatrain 62

Each of these quatrains reveals to us particular spiritual truths. The body is just a robe worn by the heart, and the whole universe is like a Sufi lodge to train our hearts. The Sufi has a language beyond the conventional concepts of heaven and hell, beyond the religion of fear. And lastly, leave the shallow stream of your ego and flow into a river deep and wide, and so transcend the repetitive drudgery of the ox pulling a plow, the tedium of soulless economic life.

Every aspect of life deserves to be sacralized in light of the sacred. The sacred is that which transmits to us something of this realm of absolute and eternal value. Seeing everything under the light of the Eternal is a way of conceiving how we might live according to our highest values. If we remember to ask ourselves what we truly value and what we hold sacred, we will deepen in our sense of purpose and continually realign with possibilities of meaning and beauty.

How Culture Is Degraded

Throughout human history, certain human beings have experienced this highest Truth and communicated its essence as much as they were able. These "completed human beings" have left a qualitative imprint on human life by their example and their words. Sometimes, too, they have developed methodologies by which others might also reach to their attainments, perceive what they perceived, and be transformed as they were transformed.

Our postmodern culture is one of doubt and cynicism, a culture that has lost a sense of meaningful coherence and so most of its art forms are expressions of incoherence, dissolution, meaninglessness, cynicism. You only need to walk through a typical art museum, viewing the quality of craft, skill, harmony, and humanness, until you get to the twentieth century and are faced with "art" virtually indistinguishable from what a child, monkey, or machine might create. It is difficult to explain this descent, but it is almost as if our human faculties have been intentionally degraded. One might conclude that in the twentieth century, culture became a mirror reflecting society's disintegration, dominated by a modernist faction that prized "originality" over all other qualities and led much of our culture down a primrose path, forsaking skill, craft, and taste for a fashionable incoherence and ugliness.

This is a good example of how culture can be degraded when it loses its connection to higher values and is debased by faddishness, commercialism, and neurotic individuality.

But let us turn back to the creative power of spirituality, which has often been the catalyst for higher civilizations.

Human beings who have experienced communion with the spiritual nature of reality offer insights into the primary sources of religion (Qur'an, Gospels, Torah, Psalms, Buddhist sutras, Vedas). To the extent that these beings have been illuminated by Universal Intelligence, they reveal a knowledge that connects us with that highest Truth, which we experience as the sacred.

Sufism, guided as it is by revelation and inspired wisdom, is ideally and at its best an expression of Universal Intelligence. The essential attribute of Universal Intelligence is, however, not something of an abstract, impersonal nature but an overwhelming sense of beauty, generosity, mercy, and love.

A human being who aspires to embody spiritual intelligence would do well to continually hold the question: "Are my thoughts, emotions, and actions in accord with my highest understanding of the good, the true, and the beautiful?" Or to put it even more simply: "Am I willing to commit to live up to my highest understanding and to reach beyond it?"

The Heart, a Source of Qualitative Knowledge

From a relatively young age, I had the sense that there was a way of knowing that was unnamed and generally unrecognized by the people around me. I searched the literature of philosophy and psychology and found only hints of this higher-order knowing. When I found the path of Sufism, I encountered the Turkish word *gönül*, which I would translate as "heart-mind." A Turk would understand that the heart and mind function as one, not two. This is gönül.

As I reflected more, asking, "What is it that the heart knows," I gradually came to realize that we live not just in the five-senses world of time and space but that we also live in a parallel reality of qualities. In Islam these qualities are referred to as Divine Names (*asma*) and Divine Attributes (*sifat*).

The realm of qualities is the dimension of value, and the heart is the assessor of value, the qualitative knower. We are already functioning with this knowing to some extent, but we are relatively unconscious of it, and we have little conscious understanding of how it might be developed.

Spirituality is a qualitative rather than a quantitative area of knowledge. Nevertheless, it is a kind of knowledge that has its own perceptive faculties and laws.

Every form of intelligence has its own essential discipline. The discipline of science is to make observations, develop hypotheses, design experiments, and so forth. Science, for instance, need not explicitly affirm spiritual principles, but to the extent that science denies or ignores the possibility of spiritual perception, it is incomplete. Such a science deals purely with quantitative and sensory realities, to the exclusion of the fact of consciousness itself.

Consciousness is the a priori fact of our existence, and what we experience in consciousness is, in addition to the world of the senses, an inner world of experience, meaning, and values. The spiritual heart is a dimensionless point, a singularity of consciousness through which consciousness gains access to the spiritual qualities inherent in the dimension of Being.

The spiritual heart is the organ of perception that enables us to have an inner experience of value. That inner experience has countless degrees or stations; it is a never-ending spiritual journey into the presence of God. A religious practice that is merely a belief in dogma or a pious performance of rituals has neglected the reality of faith and has hardly taken the first step of the spiritual journey.

Sufism is meant to purify and train the heart so that we might continually be guided by spiritual intelligence.

The Prophet Muhammad said, "Faith is a *knowledge of the heart*, a voicing with the tongue, and an action with the limbs." Faith is not mere "belief" but a state informed by an inner spiritual intelligence that informs our words, our actions, and all our human relationships.

Rumi also compares the situation of a human being to that of a blind camel that is drawn this way and that by a toggle it can't see. It does not know whether the one doing the drawing is good or bad and so continues on in heedlessness. Most people only act because they are drawn unconsciously by unseen forces.

When spiritual intelligence is lacking in a human being, signs of tension, disharmony, and discord will be apparent. Without the ordering principle of spiritual intelligence, a person's focus is easily disrupted, and personal will only exists in the pursuit of self-interest.

But if we can make the increasingly purified heart our spiritual compass, we have an astonishing way of navigating through life.

The Finer Senses

Having understood that the heart is a knowing substance, a cognitive organ that perceives qualitatively, we may better understand what Rumi has to say about our finer senses. The heart is not one thing but a nexus of subtle, subconscious faculties.

> Can you see how your bat-like senses
> are running toward the sunset,
> while your finer senses are heading toward sunrise?
> The way of physical sense perception is the way of donkeys.
> We should be ashamed of competing with other donkeys,
> jostling, nudging, and braying. You can ride another steed!
> Besides these five leaden physical senses,
> there are five golden spiritual senses.
> The bodily sense is consuming the food of darkness
> and will ultimately be consumed by what it tries to feed on;
> while the spiritual sense is feeding from a hidden Sun.
>
> *Mathnawi* II, 47–52

If, besides the animal senses, we did not have a bit of heaven within us, then would human nature have any dignity? Isn't our true value derived from our ability to connect to this pure dimension of spiritual qualities? How should the children of Adam have been honored to know the spiritual mysteries if they did not contain the Mysterion as their own intrinsic meaning?

At the heart of our tradition is an awareness of the dignity of being human. As this awareness of the value of dignity is lost, humanness is degraded by decadence in fashion, by vulgar or indecent behaviors, and by anything that debases human nature.

In the gatherings and ceremonies of traditional Sufis, appropriate dress was customary, and this dress would be in a style that would preserve a sense of the dignity of each individual—generally, loose-fitting, flowing fabrics and usually something worn on the head, whether fabric wound around the head, a turban, a scarf, or even a beret. In some orders, the *taj*, which literally means "crown" but does not resemble the crowns of royalty, would suggest that we all are of Divine origin. And yet dignity and modesty complement each other, and extravagance in dress would be out of place. In the whirling ritual of Sema especially, the ceremonial robes are a form of self-effacement in which individual personality is deemphasized with everyone dressed uniformly.

In our contemporary "secular world culture," clothing broadcasts brands, logos, commercial slogans. Sometimes the fabric is artificially shredded or faded, and perhaps even self-consciously ill-fitting. That is the common "culture."

But sometimes, too, even friends on the spiritual path neglect to respect their appearance in everyday life. Would our tradition take so much care in the preparation of sacred space and ritual only to be blind to what we individually wear? I remember one beloved dervish, a man who would be at the ready for any need, generous in any situation, and refined in his behavior, but he habitually wore an old baseball cap stained with oil and dirt. I simply raised the question, "If your head is the center of your intelligence and senses, and you are the 'crown of creation,' created as the Qur'an says in the most 'beautiful proportions,' should you not show respect to your own head in what you put on it?"

Yes, appearances are secondary and can even be deceptive, but the work of becoming human, of purifying the soul, and being the custodian of consciousness suggests that we give respect to outer form as well.

There's a further principle that is a matter of spiritual intelligence and perception, namely that design, pattern, and symbol all have spiritual effects. Someone with enough insight might recognize that certain articles of clothing, for many possible reasons, carry a vibration, have an effect, and can contribute positively or negatively to our health and spiritual well-being. If we consciously exist in "sacred space," then everything is a sign.

> You know the value of every article of merchandise,
> but if you don't know the value of your own soul,
> it's all foolishness.
> You've come to know the fortunate and the inauspicious stars,
> but you don't know whether you yourself
> are fortunate or unlucky.
> This, this is the essence of all sciences—
> that you should know who you will be
> when the Day of Reckoning arrives.
>
> *Mathnawi* III, 2652–54

Patience Is the Key

It's no crime to be blind; but if we have vision, we would do well to patiently persevere in purifying it. Patience, the last of the Ninety-Nine Names of God, is the key. The medicine of patience will burn away the veils over our eyes. Patience will open our heart to inner knowledge.

When the mirror of our heart becomes clear and pure, we will behold images that are outside of the world of water and earth. As Rumi says, "We will behold both the images and the Image-Maker, both the carpet of the spiritual empire and the One who spreads that carpet" (*Mathnawi* II, 73).

Patience is needed on the spiritual journey because we are subject to time. Impatience only sets us back on our journey. Sometimes we need to experience delays in our spiritual journeying. Time is needed for the grapes to become wine. Rumi gives this example:

Intervals are needed in order that
the blood might turn to milk
Just as a mother's blood does not become sweet milk
until she has the fortune of giving birth to a child.

Mathnawi II, 1–2

We, too, must give birth to the child of Soul. Afterward the milk
of pure spiritual knowledge begins to flow.

Patience is essential to spiritual intelligence; it completes our
listening and our seeing. The one who watches and listens with
patience will be given understanding upon understanding,
knowledge upon knowledge. As the Qur'an says, "And We will
surely test you with something of fear and hunger and a loss of
wealth and lives and fruits, but give good tidings to the patient."

Qur'an, 2:155

They will be educated directly by the Unseen, and they will find
that they have answers to questions that they could not imagine. The
Unseen will work through them and instruct others. Through patience, spiritual perception will deepen, understanding will increase,
and one will see less and less fault in the world. Nothing negative
needs to be denied or repressed. Rather than being denied or repressed, when held in the light of spiritual awareness, every negative
can be transformed by love into something positive or into an opportunity to strive for the positive.

Then the sacred will eventually suffuse and saturate every aspect
of existence. All of existence will become more and more transparent to Divine Being—in other words, we will see and experience all
of life, every circumstance, event, and relationship under the light
of the Eternal. Such an organizing principle tends toward harmony,
beauty, order, and meaning while allowing for freedom, creativity,
and wonder.

Spiritual intelligence has many levels, but I am forever grateful for the ancient knowledge passed down from heart to heart that resulted in the possibility of the highest knowledge that comes from "Spirit plus *nothing*." The Spirit is endowed with pure knowing; it is beyond Arabic, Persian, Turkish, or any human language. The one who asserts the transcendence of God and the one who asserts His immanence are bewildered by the One who, without any image or external appearance, is nevertheless appearing in all forms.

Perceiving the Oneness of Existence

Rumi says,

> How should the pure spirit of the invisible see any fault?
> Fault arises in the ignorant mind of the creature,
> not in relation to the Lord of Benevolence.
> The possibility of denial, of faithlessness (*kufr*)
> is from the wisdom of the Creator, but when it is our choice,
> it is a terrible thing.
>
> *Mathnawi* I, 1995

This last sentence is mysterious. It's a sentence spoken from the heart of Oneness. The fault lies with whoever sees nothing but faults.

The Qur'anic term *kufr*, often translated as "unbelief" or "infidelity," is that tendency of the human being to be in denial, to be stubbornly resistant to reality, and worse, to rationalize all that proceeds from that denial.

Rumi is saying that even kufr is from the wisdom of the Creator, but if we choose kufr through our own free will it is something terrible. Yet if there were not the contraries of denial and faith, kufr and *iman* (faith), we would not be tested in this world. We would not know the truth nor the beauty of existence without these polarities. So faults do exist in the world. But if we get caught up in the melodrama of blaming, we are only revealing our own faultiness.

An important term in the Mevlevi vocabulary is *Safânazar*. It is defined by Abdulbaki Golpinarli in "Mevlevî Ādāb and Customs":

Clear glance; clean, purified, serene look. These words describe the *murshid*'s (mature spiritual guide) glance at the *sâlik* (seeker), and how the *sâlik* should strive to look at everything and everyone with an eye that knows unity. The *sâlik* should not look at anything with a darkened glance (*kem nazar*) or see things in a negative light as "bad" or "worthless"; he should see everything as appropriate according to its receptivity (*mazhar*) and aptitude (*isti'dad*). In this way, the *sâlik* will continually be in the presence of God—he will be contemplating the manifestations of God— and the eventual result will be the realization of unity (*wahdet*).[3]

The Sufi learns to look at the world with two eyes, the eye of oneness and the eye of discernment. As we know from our physical eyes, it takes two eyes to have a sense of perspective. With only one eye the world is flattened.

The eye of oneness allows us to see existence, the world, as being a perfect Divine manifestation. Everything is in order, and if there is the appearance of imperfection, it is for us to work with, to be challenged by, to learn from.

The other eye, the eye of discernment, is trained upon ourselves. Though we find no fault in the outer world, we discern the difference between better and worse within ourselves. We must know ourselves with compassion, but we must also see ourselves objectively: "Am I doing my best? Am I being honest? Am I being true to my path?"

12

Spiritual Perception

IF SPIRITUAL INTELLIGENCE is our faculty for sensing the sacred and knowing our place in the universe, spiritual perception is a more focused skill, an exercising of our faculties of spiritual intelligence. In the vocabulary of Sufism, there are terms for these faculties: *kashf* (intuition), *firasa* (insight), and *marifah* (gnosis).

Since time immemorial, human beings have sought guidance and wisdom through omens and divination, reading signs in the book of nature, reflecting on proverbs, finding the deeper meanings of sacred texts. Are such activities merely superstitious? Are they remnants of a premodern mind that is incapable of thinking rationally? Or do we live in a universe that is as much meaning as it is material? Might every detail of the physical universe in some way reflect a meaning that can be read? Might all of manifested life be a book to be read? And finally, might there be a greater unifying significance and purpose to our lives that can only be adequately grasped through the subtleties of spiritual perception?

If, on the one hand, we concede that there are such things as shallow and senseless superstitions, imaginary beliefs about good and bad luck—rabbits' feet on key chains and black cats crossing our paths—then, on the other hand, we will probably recognize that some perceptions of life contain more truth than others. We will probably have experienced moments when we saw or understood in a new way, moments when life took on a deeper significance. These may be moments of dramatic crisis, overwhelming beauty, or selfless love, when the events of life seem to have intense meaning and purpose.

These are in contrast to those times when life seems to go on without purpose, when we ourselves are absorbed in the frustrating struggles, the shallow melodramas, the banalities of everyday life. But the yearning and willingness to look deeper, to seek an experience of greater truth, is what opens the door to spiritual perceptions. In other words, we can live our lives in such a way that we view all experience from a spiritual perspective.

> O You who make demands within me like an embryo,
> since You are the one who makes the demand,
> make its fulfillment easy;
> show the way, help me,
> or else relinquish Your claim
> and take this burden from me!
> Since from a debtor You're demanding gold,
> give him gold in secret, O rich King!
>
> *Mathnawi* III, 1490–92

Entering the Garden of Spiritual Truth

Whether we know it or not, we all live before the gate of the garden of spiritual truth. For some, the lock upon this gate may be such sins of the soul as pride or envy. For many, the barrier, mentioned by Rumi, is the fixation on the mouth, the stomach, or the genitals. While these are a natural part of life and can be in service to the soul, if these urges become our masters, we are blinded to the garden of spiritual realities.

When we find ourselves with a mind overpopulated with anxieties and fears, a mind scanning for anything that might threaten its happiness and survival, such a mind will be unaware, living in a narrow and distorted reality, and unreceptive to grace and guidance. Not only will it be difficult to perceive the subtler aspects of life but it will also very likely overlook and fail to appreciate what is right in front of it. Tormented by contradictory desires, absorbed by its own thought processes, confused by its own inner arguments, it will be less open to its own intuitive knowing. It will stumble where it should flow.

Here we are talking about a kind of self-created mental illness that deserves our compassion. The contents of the mind have taken over the soul rather than the soul harmonizing the mind. The ego has succumbed to unconscious forces.

We may not know to what extent this was a choice made deep in the soul. However, sometimes an imbalance may be an inherited condition, one that has afflicted some of the greatest artists and geniuses. To such people especially, we owe patience and compassion, knowing that these people may also have an unusual depth of perception and insight.

The more general rule, however, is to accept that we bear some responsibility for our mental health, that if not for these sensual and psychological obstructions, we could be drinking from the fountain of spiritual knowledge inside that gate of paradise. Spiritual perception is not some fantastic, otherworldly vision. It is our natural state. But what is natural becomes rare in an artificial world.

The mature realization of spiritual perception is not to be preoccupied with psychic or supernatural experiences but to have all our subtle faculties operating in harmony. To navigate the immediate choices of day-to-day living we can rely upon an inner "knowing" that is the result of reason, common sense, intuition, insight, and awareness of a higher calling. Just as a strong heart can mobilize the whole of our body when necessary, the totality of our mental-emotional-spiritual faculties can become a state of effective knowing to guide us through the changing circumstances of life.

Active Imagination

In addition to guiding our actions outwardly, our spiritual intelligence may apprehend the state of the soul symbolically. I recall a powerful dream I once had after meeting a certain teacher whose specialization was rhythm and movement. The dream was extremely simple and archetypal. I saw a double-tailed pennant attached to a pole. One end of the pennant waved in the breeze, silken with colorful hues, while the part attached to the pole was like concrete—gray and rigid. The transition from concrete to silk was continuous, almost imperceptible. This symbolized for me the process of dissolving rigidity and turning it into a beautiful flexibility—the very talent this shaikh excelled in.

In *The Knowing Heart* I wrote about the faculty of "active imagination." The idea of the active imagination as an "organ of the soul" has a history in Western mystical thought, especially in the writings of the sixteenth-century's Jacob Boehme and the eighteenth-century's Emanuel Swedenborg. The early twentieth-century psychoanalyst Carl Jung employed a technique called active imagination, which was an attempt to translate the contents of one's unconscious into images, symbols, or narratives. In Sufism, however, we are less concerned with giving expression to the unconscious, focusing instead on the soul's capacity to read the signs of Divine manifestation, to glimpse the presence of Divine Grace in everyday life. This is some of what I wrote in *The Knowing Heart*:

> When it is proposed that modern man has lost his soul, one meaning is that we have lost our ability to perceive through the Active Imagination which operates in an intermediate world, an interworld between the senses and the world of ideas. This Active Imagination is the imaginative, perceptive faculty of the soul, which cannot be explained because it is itself the revealer of meaning and significance. The Active Imagination does not produce some arbitrary concept standing between us and "reality," but functions directly as an organ of perception and knowledge just as real as—if not more real than—the sense organs. And its property will be that of transmuting and raising sensory data to the purity of the subtle, spiritual world.
>
> Through the Active Imagination the things and beings of

the earth will be seen in their spiritual significance. This imagination does not construct something imaginary, it unveils the hidden reality. It helps to return the facts of this world to their spiritual significance, to see beyond the apparent and to manifest the hidden. Every form is both a concealer of Truth and a possible distraction, as well as a revealer of Truth, a sign of God. Reading God's signs is an aspect of our communication with God. We can read God's signs if we learn to return the signs to their original source, to first principles.

The function of this power of the soul is in restoring a space that sacralizes the ephemeral, earthly state of being. It unites the earthly manifestation with its counterpart on the imaginal level, and raises it to incandescence.[1]

Spiritual perception is not about psychic awareness, seeing the djinn world, foretelling future events, nor a glimpse into a hidden realm of supernatural beings. It is, rather, a felt sense that we live in a beneficent and purposeful reality, an awareness of an agency beyond conventional cause and effect.

Day and night there is movement of foam on the Sea.
You see the foam, but not the Sea. Amazing!
We are dashing against each other like boats:
our eyes are darkened though we're in clear water.
O you who've gone to sleep in the body's boat,
you've seen the water,
but look at the Water of the water.
The water has a Water that is driving it;
the spirit has a Spirit that is calling it.

Mathnawi III, 1271–74

To discover that underlying ground of Being is an experience of affirmation and blessing.

117

Spiritual Perception Transforms the Perceiver

As was described in the previous chapter, what occupies most people in the contemporary world most of the time is a superficial search for love, pleasure, and security. To the extent that someone may search for knowledge, it is most often not the knowledge of the sacred but rather a knowledge of external things and the means to effect change in the material or social realm. Our innate intelligence is reduced to a mere problem-solving, strategizing faculty.

Yet to understand the nature and purpose of our spiritual intelligence and its capacity for spiritual perception is vitally important to our fundamental well-being and happiness. Spiritual perception transforms the perceiver.

Every human being carries an inheritance of spiritual intelligence, which is the reflection of the Universal Intellect on the human level. The particular, individualized intellect of each human being is potentially a portal for the streaming of the Universal Intellect, the awesome intelligence that nourishes our individual intellect.

From the Quranic perspective, this intelligence was a faculty implanted in Adam, the archetypal human being and the first "prophet." Spiritual perception grants the ability to discern the absolute from the relative—in other words, to be able to view existence in the widest possible perspective, in a context so vast so as to see even the most ordinary and transient things bathed in the light of eternity.

The purpose of our innate intelligence is to know reality adequately, objectively, totally. Spiritual perception is to glimpse the Divine within this mundane existence. We are equipped by our very nature to be able to perceive many qualities of the Divine, many levels of reality, and to experience a state of well-being and peace by communing with a Presence that is always here, no matter what our outer circumstances may be.

It is a firm and reliable principle that communion with the Divine lessens the power of the false self. It melts the ice of the false self and allows the fluid water of soul to flow. This intimacy and communion with spiritual reality is the most satisfying experience possible for a human being. In the end it will be recognized as the very purpose of our lives.

The result of this communion is a state of spaciousness, an opening to awe and wonder, an induced humility and gratitude, and, finally, a beauty of character fulfilled in action.

Anyone, to the degree of his enlightenment,
sees as much as he has polished of himself.
The more she polishes, the more she sees,
the more visible do the forms become.
If you say purity is by the grace of God,
this success in polishing is also through that generosity.
That work and prayer is in proportion to the yearning:
people have nothing but what they have striven for.

Mathnawi IV, 2909–12

This last condition—beautiful character in action—is one of the highest fulfillments for a human being. Character is not only harmonizing our self with the highest Truth but also simultaneously engaging dynamically in life.

Spiritual perception is realized and developed through our engagement with the conditions we find ourselves in. There is purpose in our being embodied here. It is in facing the challenges and sufferings of life that the soul awakens into true intelligence and, with it, greater love.

The Influence of the Spiritually Transformed

The perceptive soul is the fully human soul. The human being who lives every moment aware of the spiritual significance of our relationships, obligations, and possibilities becomes a living presence that radiates blessing and transforms the circumstances of everyday life.

Great civilizations, immortal artistic achievements, and moral systems that have elevated human life have originated with spiritually transformed human beings. Hermes, Plato, Pythagoras, Zoroaster, Confucius, Lao Tzu, Jesus, Muhammad, Francis of Assisi, Rumi—such souls have birthed cultures and civilizations. The rich Sufi culture of Muslim India was created in the intimate circle of Nizamuddin Awliya and Amir Khusraw. Its music and poetry, musical instruments, and ceremonial aspects, created in the fourteenth century, are still alive, and the great qawwali singer Nusrat Fateh Ali Khan was the most popular singer in the world when he passed away in 1997.

The spiritually perceptive soul resonates with the vibration of higher knowledge, a knowledge that is also a kind of energy. Higher knowledge is available when we resonate at the frequency of that knowledge. It is highly unlikely that someone who is living at the frequency of coarser, mundane interests, whose primary focus is the accumulation of power and possessions, will gain access to spiritual perception and higher knowledge.

On the other hand, when higher knowledge is experienced, it is as if it was revealed from above, not built up from below by deductive reasoning. Such knowledge is a gift of heaven after which we can never be the same as before.

> No mirror ever became iron again;
> no bread ever became wheat;
> no ripened grape ever became sour fruit.
> Mature yourself and be secure
> from a change for the worse.
> Become the Light.
>
> *Mathnawi* II, 1317–8

Spiritual perception is not merely some kind of information; it is not an accumulation of facts. Spiritual perception, to one degree or another, can awaken extraordinary human faculties. Rumi tells us to consider the story of Solomon and the Farthest Mosque where plants would appear and reveal their healing properties to him:

The Intellect whose sight does not rove ('aql-i má zágh)
is the light of the elect; the crow-like intellect ('aql-i zágh)
is the sexton for the spiritually dead.
The spirit that flies after crows—
the crow carries it toward the graveyard.
Beware! Do not run in pursuit of the crow-like fleshly soul,
for it takes you to the graveyard, not toward the orchard.
If you go, go in pursuit of the 'Anqá of the heart,
toward the Qáf and Farther Mosque of the heart.
With every moment of your contemplation
a new plant is growing in your own "Farther Mosque."
Like Solomon, give it its due: investigate it, do not reject it,
do not trod it under foot, because the various sorts of plants
declare to you the inward state of this firm earth.
Whether in the earth there are sugarcanes or only common
       reeds,
every soil of the earth is interpreted by its plants.
Therefore the heart's soil, of which thought was always the
       plant—
those thoughts have revealed the heart's secrets.
If in a gathering I find someone that draws
the discourse from me toward themselves,
I, like the garden, will grow hundreds of thousands of roses.

Mathnawi IV, 1309–15

Here Rumi takes us into the consciousness of a prophet, Solomon, whose attention does not waver and who is living in a reality imbued with meaning. A true prophet is the embodiment of spiritual intelligence, an inheritor and reflector of the Universal Intellect. Solomon can read the signs of nature like a shaman, aware of the healing properties of particular plants. But Rumi takes it a step further, drawing an analogy between the properties of particular soils and the fertile ground of the human heart that yields up the thought content of the psyche. He also remarks on the dynamic relationship between human beings—the ability, for instance, of a receptive listener to draw out beautiful discourses from a speaker.

A Prophet Embodies Universal Intellect

In the Islamic worldview, messengers (*rasuls*) and prophets (*nabis*) have been sent to countless human communities and have been the recipients of objective knowledge about the nature of reality and the purpose of human life. The *rasul* brings an original message, a moral code, a revelation from Divine Intelligence, while the *nabi* may be one in a religious lineage, like many of the Hebrew prophets. Both messengers and prophets are human beings like us, except that they have a prophetic function to fulfill, a mission to exemplify a higher aspect of humanness. They distinguish themselves from the masses of humanity who are lost in conjecture and opinion. Unlike so many human beings whose consciousness is distorted from being under the domination of a false self, a counterfeit identity, the prophets are examples of a purified consciousness capable of reflecting Universal Intelligence.

Such prophets, among indigenous peoples for instance, may have been known only within their own local community and even eventually lost in the shadows of time. Sometimes, too, they are at the fountainhead of a new religion or even an entire culture. Three primary practices of the First Peoples of North America—the peace pipe, the sweat lodge, and respect for the feminine—trace back to White Buffalo Calf Woman of the Lakota Sioux.

These prophets and messengers bring a refreshing, reorienting, even revolutionary perspective into the darkness of societal ignorance and delusion. They can inform us about the true possibilities of our lives.

How many idols did Ahmad (Muhammad) break in the world,
that the religious communities might cry "O Lord"!
Had it not been for the efforts of Ahmad, you also,

like your ancestors, would be worshipping idols.
This head of yours has been delivered from bowing to idols
in order that you may acknowledge his rightful claim
upon the (gratitude of the religious) communities.
If you speak, speak thanks for this deliverance
that he may also deliver you from the idol within.
Since he has delivered your head from idols, deliver
your heart also by means of that strength.

Mathnawi II, 366–70

The Prophet Muhammad received his first revelation while on retreat in a cave outside Mecca. The night of the first revelation is known as "The Night of Power." It was as if on that one night, he received the essence of what would be revealed on discrete occasions over the next twenty-three years. The revelation began with these words:

Recite, in the name of your Sustainer who created,
created the human being from a germ-cell.
Truly, your Lord is the Most Generous,
Who taught with the Pen,
taught the human being what it did not know.

Surah al-'Alaq 96:1–5

The very first communication from this Infinite Intelligence, this Sustainer, Educator, and Lord, was the gift of knowledge revealed through a cosmic Pen, which some commentators say symbolizes the Universal Intellect. The essence of the Divine/human relationship is educational—the sharing of objective, metaphysical knowledge about what is of absolute value.

The kind of knowledge that is attained through intellectual speculation, or through building conceptual systems, is one kind of knowledge. But spiritual knowledge is given in a flash, from a higher world, received by the heart and only later perhaps understood by the intellect.

Some people imitate Muhammad in what they imagine to be his dress and behavior, but the Persian poet and mystic Shams of Tabriz tells us,

> Obeying Muhammad is to follow him when he experiences *Lay-lat al-Miraj*.[2] Work so that you have a place in their hearts. If you desire only the world and work only for this world, you will be among the losers. If you search within the religion, you won't lose. Then you will worship, look for Haqq (Reality), and follow the path of lovers of Haqq.[3]

For Rumi and his mentor Shams, Muhammad held a unique position, as the completion of the historical cycle of revelation and as a beloved exemplar. Muhammad inspired both of them, not only with the knowledge he received—namely, the Qur'an—but through his noble character, which became a model all Sufis would try to live up to.

Among Muhammad's many qualities is his steadfast integrity. During the early years of his prophethood, he was offered wealth, women, even kingship, all of which he refused rather than betray the call his heart had received. Rumi tells us,

> The Prophet's soul has no friend except God:
> he has nothing to do with the acceptance or rejection of the
>   people.
> The reward for delivering the Divine message comes from God:
> Notwithstanding that he is hated
> or seen as an enemy for the Beloved's sake.
>
> *Mathnawi* III, 2930

People will perceive, know, and understand Muhammad only as much as they are able, only as much as their hearts are illuminated and freed from narrow prejudices. Some despised him; some gave their hearts to him.

> Abú Jahl saw Muhammad and said,
> "He's an ugly figure that was born from the sons of Háshim!"
> Muhammad said to him, "You are right,
> you have spoken truth, although you are impertinent."
> The Siddíq (Abú Bakr) saw him and said,
> "O Sun, you are neither of East nor of West: shine beautifully!"
> Muhammad said, "You have spoken the truth, dear friend,
> O you that have escaped from this world of nothingness."
> Those that were present said, "O King, why did you call both of
>   them truth-tellers when they contradicted each other?"
> He replied, "I am a mirror polished by the Divine hand:
> whether Turcoman or Indian, each sees in me
> that which exists in themselves."
>
> *Mathnawi* I, 2365–70

An ignorant and hateful person will give one description of him based on their darkness and preconceptions. Good-hearted people will admire or even fall in love with him. A few may experience some degree of the transformation that Muhammad called them to.

> You avoid giving thanks for your religion,
> you don't praise Allah for being born a Muslim.
> You don't know the value of the religion that Muhammad
> brought to you because you didn't expend any effort for it.
> You received your religion from your father as an inheritance.
>
> *Mathnawi* I, 371–72

Seeing Through Muhammad's Eyes

To truly know a prophet requires that we be cleansed of our egoistic desires and prejudices, including all self-righteousness, fanaticism, and tribalism. Perhaps to truly know the Prophet Muhammad would be to increase in the qualities of spiritual perception that he had:

> To the Prophet, this world is plunged in glorification of God,
> while to many it looks inanimate.
> To his eye this world is filled with abundant love;
> to the eyes of others it is inert and lifeless.
> To his eye, valley and hill are in fluid motion:
> he hears subtle discourses from sod and bricks.
> To the vulgar, this whole world is a corpse in chains:
> Is there any veil of blindness more incredible than this?
>
> *Mathnawi* IV, 3532–35

This capacity for spiritual perception is the result of the union of self with Spirit. Through communion with the Mysterion, the self is purified and transformed. This vision is not the result of a process of human thought as much as it is a gift, given after we have humbled ourselves enough to receive it. Muhammad himself indicated this when he said, in all humility, "My Lord, I have not known You as You deserve to be known."

We need to ask for knowledge from the Source of Knowledge. This is one of the lessons we learn from him, just as he said, "Ya Rabb (O My God), show us the Truth as the truth and give us the blessing of following it, and show us falsehood as false and give us the blessing of avoiding it."

Seven Practices for Developing Spiritual Perception

1. Cherish our relationship with the Divine. Gratitude, humility, contrition, patience, hope, trust, intention, and love arise when we remember the true nature of the Divine. All of these qualities contribute to polishing the mirror of the heart. The polished heart is the instrument of spiritual perception.

2. Begin *now* with what is right in front of us, opening our eyes to what is. How often do we really see? How have our habits of seeing blinded us?

3. Be aware of the state of the heart. Is the heart troubled or at peace? Every day we make choices. But what is the basis of our choice? Do we make choices informed by an open heart?

4. Be alert to signs. Do we see and listen? Spiritual perception is to be empty enough to receive the guidance of the moment. Avoid overthinking it. Simply be awake to the guidance of the moment.

5. See others as souls. Respect and be sensitive to the relationships we have. The "hardened heart" sees others as "things." The awakened heart sees the animate nature of everything. When we can see the soulfulness of other human beings, we are more sensitive and that may be subtly communicated to them.

6. See more and more with the glance of the Divine. This is called in the Sufi tradition a "clear glance," a clean, purified, serene look. These words describe the murshid's glance at the seeker and how the seeker should look at everything and everyone with an eye that knows unity. The seeker should not look at anything with a darkened glance or see things in a negative light as "bad" or "worthless"; they should see everything as appropriate according to its receptivity (*mazhar*) and aptitude (*isti'dad*). In this way, the seeker (*sâlik*) will continually be in the presence of God—contemplating the manifestations of God—and the eventual result will be the realization of unity (*wahdet*).

7. Resolve to bring our actions into accord with our spiritual perception. When we act on what we know, we are given more knowledge. Virtue is choosing with self-less wisdom. Egoism chooses out of fear with self-interest in mind. Allow our spiritual perception to inform our conscious intentions.

As Rumi reminds us, the human being is essentially an eye. The eye of the heart can be veiled by the physical senses, but when the spiritual senses are awakened, even the physical senses become illumined. For this reason, the science of Sufism is also called *tasawwuf*, signifying the purification of perception.

If the Divine is the ultimate creative power, the creativity that brought us delicious fruits, fragrant roses, the spectacle of nature, and the beauties of human relationships, that same creative power has also brought us an inner life of even vaster dimensions, subtler beauties, spiritual virtues, and experiences both subtle and profound. If on the one hand the birth from the physical womb leads us into the beauties of the sensory world, a second birth from the spiritual womb brings us into a spiritual universe of awesome beauty and meaning.

Communion, the Experience of the Sacred

It is important to understand that if we talk about perfecting our souls, it is not some personal ambition. The perfection of the soul has more to do with overcoming our preoccupation with the self than with any form of personal ambition. As Rumi says, "Come to me without you and I will come to you without me."

This unhealthy preoccupation with the self, which sometimes seems such an intractable problem, can most effectively be dissolved through contact and communion with Divine Being. This is not some remote possibility meant for a few spiritual geniuses. It is, in fact, what every human being is made for. We are designed with a capability for Divine relationship, an experience of the sacred. In fact, nothing other than this communion will bring enduring peace, contentment, and true happiness. The experience of the sacred is inherently an experience of love and meaning.

It is a firm and reliable principle that some measure of communion with the Divine diminishes the false self. It melts the ice of the false self so that it becomes the fluid water of life. This communion is the very purpose of our lives and in the end the most satisfying experience possible for a human being. The result of this communion is a state of spaciousness, an opening to awe and wonder, an induced humility and gratitude, and, finally, a beauty of character fulfilled in action through love.

Communion with the Divine through the awakening of spiritual intelligence can be seen from two perspectives. From one perspective, we take the initiative; we do our best to open ourselves to the Divine and Its qualities. But from another perspective, the Divine Reality Itself acts upon our being, imbuing us, qualifying us with Its qualities. Both points of view have validity, and it would be misleading to focus on only one of these perspectives, for our yearning to encounter the Divine is the Divine's own impulse in us. If Divine communion requires, at least, that we direct our pure and sincere attention toward the Divine Radiance, the very impulse to do so is the result of some Divine action arising from within ourselves.

13

Show Us Things as They Are

DISCERNMENT IS THE THEME that holds this rambling chapter together. It's not unlike the style of Rumi's *Mathnawi*, where stories, metaphysical reflections, and poetry follow upon each other in a continual metamorphosis of meanings. Discernment exists in every area of life according to what criteria we employ. The quality of our discernment determines the outcome of many choices in life: Who will we associate with? How will we choose one thing over another? Where will we look for guidance and knowledge? Who will we trust?

I try to imagine a child born into today's world, exposed primarily to mass media and entertainment, being educated in a relatively soulless educational system, little exposed to the great traditions of literature, raised by secular parents pursuing their ambitions within the value systems of our monetized, consumerist society.

Where in today's world would such a child find adequate knowledge about the spiritual nature of reality and the potential of the human soul? And is this knowledge itself something like "an endangered species" as the lure of technocratic culture sweeps the world?

These questions are more than can be answered in the context of this work, so let us take note of the situation and focus specifically on a single question: By what criterion might we discern and evaluate what is most important for our souls? In choosing a livelihood, who to marry, where to live, what to do in our free time, or what to pray for, do we consider what would most benefit our souls?

Discernment and Spiritual Laws

Someone with little discernment stumbles through life, constantly surprised that things are not turning out as expected. A person has a "problem," and they choose a "solution" only to find that the solution has created further problems. Maybe their choices are based in appearances that should not be trusted, or in the ego's magical thinking, or under the spell of glamor (yes, even in spiritual matters), or to win others' approval at any cost. Maybe their choices are contaminated by the false values of the world.

This kind of problem is common in our personal lives and also in today's technologically innovating societies where we are encouraged to believe that every problem has a technological solution. So much of contemporary "civilization" is built on shortsighted solutions to problems created by "civilization" itself. So many human problems result from a lack of discernment regarding the well-being of the soul. We have "social media" for our depersonalized life; we have nutritional supplements to add to depleted foods; we have too many remedies that only address symptoms of compromised health rather than the knowledge of how to fundamentally maintain health.

Too often we look in all the wrong places to solve the problems of life. We abandon trust and contentment and create nonexistent problems in our minds. Because of a spiritual disconnect, the self is lost, exiled from its own inner knowing. Rumi says we chase after shadows:

A bird is flying high;
its shadow speeds over the earth like an actual bird:

a fool starts to chase the shadow,
running so far that he exhausts himself,
not knowing that it is but the reflection of that bird in the air,
not knowing where the origin of the shadow is.

He shoots arrows at the shadow and the quiver is emptied—
his life is wasted by what he seeks.

Mathnawi I, 417–22

Hunting shadows is a useless occupation. Chasing after things of no substance while being oblivious of the bird in the air is a futile waste of energy.

What is the high-flying bird and what is the shadow? Sufi metaphysics describes a level of reality of Divine Attributes of which the things of this earth are manifestations.

Rumi gives this example: Divine Beauty is like sunlight on the brick wall; the brick wall suddenly seems resplendent, but it is a borrowed splendor. If the sunlight is withdrawn, the bricks are seen in a different light. All "things" are, in a sense, symbols, and what they symbolize are those Divine Attributes. If we could enter a portal into the dimension of Divine Attributes, we would increase our capacity to manifest things, conditions, relationships that are imbued with those attributes. We would be reflecting the Divine in the manifest world.

Whereas if we chase after the shadow forms, we are neglecting the attributes at their origin. Rumi's advice is to place ourselves "under the shadow" of a true "servant of God."

But when the shadow of God tends to him,
it delivers him from every illusion.
The shadow of God is that servant of God
who has died to this world and is living through that One.
Quickly, take hold of his robe
that you may be saved during the last days of this earth.

Mathnawi I, 423–24

Spiritual Egoism

One of the dangers of the spiritual path—and here I especially mean the esoteric path—is the possibility of the prideful ego appropriating the whole process of developing higher will and consciousness. Someone may have a very high development of will and consciousness and use this development for selfish purposes. Some of these people might even exercise their egoistic ambition in the field of spirituality. What is the difference between an Aleister Crowley (an occultist magician) and a Saint Francis?

Rumi's criterion for a guide worthy of trust is quite precise: "that servant of God who has died to this world and is living through that One."

So what kind of discernment is needed in choosing a spiritual guide, a *murshid*, which means literally one who "gives guidance"? This is where, on the one hand, some people in our contemporary "egalitarian" societies are too suspicious or cynical about accepting any guidance from another human being, while others throw discernment away when they encounter a turbaned shaikh with thousands of followers, or a scholar who has written many books, or someone whose father or ancestors were famous spiritual figures.

I remember a large international Sufi conference where I unfortunately arrived a little late for a breakout session and found myself standing in the back of a crowded lecture hall. As I listened to the talk, I found the ideas true enough, but something was not quite right. The subject was the nature of love and Rumi's popularity in the West, but the emotional tone was incongruous. The tone of voice, the facial expressions, the gestalt was that of a growling dog! The room was packed with people interested in one of humanity's greatest exemplars of love, but there was no *ashq* (passionate spiritual love). I wondered how many in that room were listening with their hearts, not just their intellects.

Shams of Tabriz has something to say about the difference between those with *ashq* and those without it.

The People of Paradise and the People of Hell

Let me tell you about the qualities of the people of paradise. Let me also tell you the signs of the people of hell. . . .

Whomever you see who has a beautiful temperament and a beautiful face, if their words are straightforward, if they are openhearted and pray for good things for everyone, a joy of heart comes from the speech of such a person. Such a person makes you forget the anxieties and tightness of this universe; your inside opens in such a way that even if they swear at you, you laugh. Maybe, when they speak of unity . . . you weep, but you feel a hundred thousand joys and laughter within yourself. Such a person is a being of paradise.

There is also a kind of person who drinks blood; there is a coldness on their face and in their words that only bring you anxiety. Their words are repulsive rather than warming like the speech of the joyful human being. Well, such a person is a devil, a person of hell. Now, whoever has realized such a secret behaves accordingly and doesn't praise a hundred thousand shaikhs.[1]

To return to the subject of chasing shadows, perhaps a slightly different example found in *Fihi ma fihi* will help us understand:

I know truly the rule for God's provision, and it is not in my character to run here and there in vain or to suffer needlessly. Truly, whatever my daily portion is—of money, food, clothing, or the fire of lust—if I sit quietly, it will come to me. If I run around in search of my daily bread, the effort exhausts and demeans me. If I am patient and stay in my place, it will come to me without pain and humiliation. My daily bread is seeking me out and drawing me. When it can't draw me, it comes—just as when I can't draw it, I go to it.

The upshot of these words is that you should be so engaged in the affairs of the Way that this world will run after you. What is meant by "sitting" here is sitting on the affairs of the Way. If a man runs, when he runs for the Way he is sitting. If he is sitting, when he is sitting for this world he is running. The Prophet said, "Whoever makes all his cares a single care, God will spare him all his cares." If a man has ten concerns, let him be concerned with the Way: God will see to the other nine without his having to see to them. The prophets were not concerned with fame or bread. Their only concern was to seek God's satisfaction, and they acquired both fame and bread. Whoever seeks God's satisfaction will be with the prophets in this world and the next; he will be a companion with "those unto whom God has been gracious, of the prophets, and the sincere, and the martyrs" [*Surah an-Nisa* 4:69]. What place is this? He will be rather sitting with God, who said, "I sit next to him who remembers Me." If God were not sitting with him, there would be no desire for God in his heart. Without a rose, there is no rose scent; without musk, there is no aroma of musk. There is no end to these words, and even if there were, it would not be like the end to other words.

Signs of the Unseen [Fihi ma fihi], Discourse 49

In the situation described here, God's Providence depends on making our spiritual focus the highest priority. This requires, when possible, focusing one's whole being on the Divine Reality, and even in the midst of our everyday lives to reserve a part of our attention for God. This is a perfect example of the Mysterion, that inner essence that allows us to be intimate with God, that opens us to the mystery of this Divine Providence and intimacy.

A person who is conscious of this Mysterion will be given profound insights and perceptions. They go to the causative level, to that inner space where the Divine Attributes rule and higher thoughts and emotions are born. In that dimensionless point is the remedy for every ill, the answer to every question, the solution to every problem, the satisfaction of every need.

Those who embody the Mysterion turn away from superficial distractions, shallow entertainments, technological toys. Their awakened spiritual capacities can learn about the properties of plants directly from nature, as Solomon did. Their health is more intact because their appetites are healthy. Their hearts are alive and sustain meaningful relationships. They know that intentions, desires, and thoughts have both tangible and intangible effects. And they are more aware of their responsibility for every thought, desire, and intention.

> Vain breathings and lies can't be joined with Truth.
> O friend, you are as you think.
> As for the rest of you, it's only flesh and bone.

> If your thought is a rose, you are a rose garden;
> and if your thoughts are thorns,
> you are just kindling for the bath stove.

Mathnawi II, 277–78

The Baraka of Intention

Muhammad said, "The reward of deeds depends upon the intentions, and a person will get the rewards according to what he has intended."[2]

The fundamental importance of intention is continually affirmed in Sufi practice. The foundation of our action is the intention (*niyyah*) behind it. The niyyah is even more important than the action itself. In fact, the intention is the very spirit of the action.

I have learned over the years in my own role as a Sufi teacher that if I need to correct someone's behavior, I only give myself permission to do so if I can act with love. If the corrective might be emotionally painful but the intention is loving, there is a much greater chance for benefit.

A healer we know in Turkey has a reputation for sometimes applying rough and painful treatments. However, no one seems to complain because they experience the benefits even if their arms or legs sometimes wind up black and blue. Knowing this person for many years, I can say that there is no self-interest in his work, only love and service to God. I once heard him say to someone, "I may make you scream, but you are healed; there are some whose touch is soft and yet they make you sick."

The quality of intention behind any spiritual practice, especially the ritual prayer, determines the benefit. Every time we stand, bow, and prostrate in prayer, we are practicing showing up before the Divine Face without any self-importance, selfish strategy, or pretense. It is a continuous training in sincerity. The form of worship has little value unless we put our souls into it.

The importance of this spiritual law of intention is epitomized by this traditional Sufi saying:

Baraka (blessing) will disappear
when the intention is not right.

On the surface of it, this helps to explain why sometimes the "good actions" of certain people bring little or no benefit. The first time I heard it, these words carried a powerful effect.

The word *baraka* suggests a force of spiritual transmission, a power beyond time operating through channels of grace. Certain places could have baraka: the shrine of a saint or a sacred place in nature. A ritual or ceremony could have baraka: the Sufi ceremony of initiation (*bayat*), which connects the seeker to a living tradition of grace. Finally, a spiritual lineage sourced in a "complete human being" could be a source of baraka.

The idea that "right intention" could also be the prerequisite for the operation of such a spiritual influence caught my imagination and stirred my conscience. How often have there been times when my, or our, own lack of "right intention" had undermined the grace coming through our spiritual activities, rituals, or gatherings? I vowed to examine my own intentions, to reflect more deeply on my motives, and to seek to be more conscious of the quality of intention, especially in whatever I would undertake in the name of Sufism.

In the presence of His Glory,
closely watch your heart
so your thoughts won't shame you.

For He sees guilt, opinion, and desire
as plainly as a hair in pure milk.

Mathnawi I, 3144–45

By a single thought that comes into the mind,
in one moment a hundred worlds are overturned.

Mathnawi II, 1029

Show Us Things as They Are

One of our blessed teachers, Hasan Lutfi Shushud, referred to Sufism as "the path of verification." If our yearning is to know the Real, *al-Haqq*, we will do whatever we can to continually discern truth from falsehood. I have long been amazed at Muhammad's saying,

(O My God), show us the Truth as the truth
and give us the blessing of following it,
and show us falsehood as false
and give us the blessing of avoiding it.

Muhammad not only continually sought the truth, but he also asked to be shown the truth. Hasan Lutfi Shushud would surely agree that the best way to discern the truth from falsehood, to distinguish what is truly a blessing from what might be a curse, is to stand in humility and awe before the Divine Unknown and ask to be guided. Rumi expresses it this way:

God works in mysterious ways. Some things may look beneficial outwardly, but there may be harm within them. Let no one be deluded by conceit that he himself has birthed good ideas or has done good deeds.

If everything were as it seemed, the Prophet would not have cried out with such illuminated and illuminating insight, "Show me things as they are! You make things seem beautiful when in reality they are ugly; You make things seem ugly when in reality they are beautiful. Therefore, show us each thing as it is that we might not fall into a trap and be really in error."

Now your judgment, however good and clear it may be, is not better than Muhammad's, and he spoke as he did. Don't rely on your own thoughts and opinions but humble yourself before God and stand in awe of Him.

Signs of the Unseen [Fihi ma fihi], Discourse 1

The health of our souls depends on spiritual discernment, which is the guardian of the soul. The human being in resonance with the wider field of Being has many subtle faculties beyond the thinking brain. Reason is useful to analyze data, engineer certain solutions, and organize certain activities. Project managers and event organizers, for instance, need reason. But for a vision of human life, for qualitative decisions, for fulfilling relationships, for discovering a sense of purpose, for discerning what will benefit our souls, we would do better to orient our hearts to a dimension beyond material existence.

May the generations now being born be shown a way to the Truth and be able to discern what will benefit their souls.

14

The Messenger and the Message

The All-Merciful has taught the Qur'an.

Qur'an, *Surah ar-Rahman* 55:1–2

Now let us look at the biography of the Prophet Muhammad, peace be upon him, as the story of the individual living out a relationship with the pole of Spirit. It is the story of a person unexpectedly beginning to receive profound revelations, being rejected, boycotted, and driven out of Mecca with those who believed in him, then being aggressively attacked, having to learn to defend themselves, and finally through a moral victory triumphantly returning to Mecca without bloodshed, offering amnesty to the rebellious elements that were the cause of the hostilities. That is the outer story.

Early on, Muhammad was offered kingship and every possible privilege, if only he would give up what the establishment of his day considered unreasonable demands. The Prophet, or Messenger, must be someone who lives under Divine grace and guidance, not someone who acts in a self-serving, self-aggrandizing way. The demands he was guided to make were namely the recognition of the one universal Divine Being and the abandonment of idolatry, superstition, female infanticide, and exploitive injustice. It was not the imposition of a religion on a community but the recognition of spiritual principle and the necessary consequences of that recognition.

To thee We sent the Book [Qur'an] in truth confirming the revelations that came before it and guarding it in safety; so judge between them by what Allah has revealed and follow not their vain
desires diverging from the truth that has come to you. To each
among you have We prescribed a Law and an Open Way. If Allah
had so willed, He would have made you a single people, but you
will be put to the test in what He has given you: so strive as in a
race in all virtues. The goal of you all is to Allah; it is He that will
show you the truth of the matters in which you dispute.

Surah al-Maʿidah 5:48

To give one example of how Muhammad continually sought
guidance in prayer:

Abu Huraira reported: The Messenger of Allah, peace and blessings be upon him, said, "O Allah, set right my religion that is a
guardian of my affairs, set right my worldly life in which is my
livelihood, and set right my Hereafter that is my place of return.

Ṣaḥīḥ Muslim 2720

This noble soul who would profoundly change the course of
history did not presume that he already had sufficient wisdom unto
himself but would humbly pray for guidance. This overarching sup-
plication would be repeated regularly as a kind of fail-safe in his role
as leader, spiritual guide, and even as a human being. Once established in the humility of that relationship, he could enter into active
life and trust that knowledge and guidance would be given.

In the Prophet Muhammad, we have the embodiment not of
some superhuman ideal but of a human being who strived to be a
true and faithful servant. He oriented himself faithfully to the divine pole of his inner being. Chosen by the Divine, he expressed wisdom countless times with an economy of language that continues to
inspire:

He who humbles himself for the sake of God, him will God exalt; he is small in his own mind, and great in the eyes of the people. And he who is proud and haughty, God will render him contemptible, and he is small in the eyes of the people and great in his own mind.

"Forgive him who wrongs you; join him who cuts you off; do good to him who does evil to you and speak the truth even if it be against yourself." (These words were said to be found inscribed on the hilt of the Prophet's sword.)

Muhammad accumulated neither wealth nor material privilege for himself or his family. When he died, although he was the leader of a large community, all he owned was a reed mat to sleep on and a block of wood for a pillow. He appeared before his people shortly before his death and his most important question was: "Have I delivered to you without distortion the message I was given by God?"

The Criterion, the Discernment, al-Furqan

The Qur'an is sometimes referred to as "the Criterion" (al-Furqan). Among its purposes is offering direction and counsel in regard to our earthly and eternal lives. Its guidance is not meant to be dogmatic but revelatory. Whether as intimations of guidance or warning, it offers spiritual principles not to be merely believed but to be verified in one's experience in order to become effective in one's life. "Indeed, in the remembrance of God hearts find tranquility" (Surah ar-Ra'd 13:28) is one of those revelatory principles that can be put to the test.

For Rumi, the Qur'an's guidance is moral and spiritual in nature. He understood Islam as a system for spiritual perfection, not a political ideology. Nor does Rumi claim that the Qur'an has an exclusive claim to Truth. On the contrary, he suggests that someone who recognizes the spiritual truth of the Qur'an will be able to recognize that same truth wherever it occurs.

God's treasure houses are many, and God's knowledge is vast.
If a man knowledgeably reads *one* Qur'an, why should he reject
any *other* Qur'an? I once said to a Qur'an reader, "The Qur'an
says, 'Say, "If the sea were ink to write the words of my Lord, truly the sea would fail, before the words of my Lord would fail"'"
(*Surah al-Kahf* 18:109).

Signs of the Unseen [*Fihi ma fihi*], Discourse 18

Here the Qur'an affirms the unlimited nature of Divine revelations and signs—in nature, in human nature, in every detail of existence. Far from claiming to be an exclusive and limited source of
Truth, the Qur'an affirms the vast scope of Divine communication;
its inclusivity is evidence of its universal truth.

And yet not everyone who reads and believes in the Qur'an benefits from it. What accounts for people's ability or inability to receive
and act on such guidance?

According to Rumi, at the time of the Prophet, those who had
memorized even a few lines of the Qur'an were much admired because they digested the essence of it, while in later days there are
many who have memorized the whole of the Qur'an and have bene-
fited little. It is about such that it is said, "Many a reader of the Qur'an
is cursed by the Qur'an" (*Signs of the Unseen* [*Fihi ma fihi*], Discourse
65)—that is, one who is not aware of its real meaning.

As for those who are actively seeking to understand this revelation but are encountering resistance, confusion, or sheer bewilder-
ment, Rumi has this advice:

The Qur'an is like a shy bride. Although you try to pull aside her
veil, she will not show you her face. The reason you have no pleasure or discovery in all your study of it is that it rejects your attempt to pull off its veil. It tricks you and shows itself to you as
ugly, as if to say, "I am not that beauty." It is capable of showing
any face it wants. If, on the other hand, you do not tug at the veil,

144

but you acquiesce, give water to its sown field, do it service from afar and try to do what pleases it without pulling at its veil, it will show you its face. Seek the people of God, "Enter among my servants; and enter my paradise" (*Surah al-Fajr* 89:29–30).

Signs of the Unseen [*Fihi ma fihi*], Discourse 65

Form, Substance, and Spiritual Nuance

One of the crucial spiritual principles to be integrated into our souls is the discernment of substance beyond form. Sometimes it seems that certain people are "locked up" in their opinions and preconceptions, impenetrable to spiritual beauty and truth:

> It strikes me as odd how anyone who has memorized the Qur'an is unable to penetrate the state of the mystics. . . .
>
> The Qur'an is an amazingly jealous piece of magic. It contrives to say frankly in an opponent's ear what he understands but cannot comprehend or take any delight in. If it were otherwise, it would snatch him away, but "God hath sealed up (their hearts and their hearing)" (*Surah al-Baqarah* 2:7). What a wondrous grace God has to set a seal on those who hear without understanding and who deliberate without understanding. God is gracious, His wrath is gracious, and His "locking up" is gracious; yet unlike His locking up is His "unlocking," the graciousness of which is beyond description.

Signs of the Unseen [*Fihi ma fihi*], Discourse 35

The Subtlety of Spiritual Discernment

In Rumi's time and culture there was little need to convince people of the genuineness of the Qur'an as spiritual guidance, but there was a great need to illuminate the profound meanings to be discovered there.

Everybody has his own way of doing things. The Qur'an is a two-sided brocade. Although some benefit from one side of it and some from the other, they are both right because God wants both groups to derive benefit. It is like a woman who has a husband and also a nursing infant: each derives a different pleasure from her: the infant from the milk in her breasts, and the husband from being married to her. People who take external pleasure from the Qur'an and "drink its milk" are "infants of the Way," but those who have attained perfection have a different enjoyment and understanding of the meaning of the Qur'an.

Signs of the Unseen [*Fihi ma fihi*], Discourse 44

Rumi is obviously not prudish in giving us this example. It is a masterful way to tell us that there is an immature understanding and a mature understanding of the Qur'an.

What he has to say about discovering these deeper meanings applies not just to the Qur'an but to the fabric of reality as a whole. What distinguishes the path of Sufism from the path of blind faith is that one engaged in following the Sufi path is operating on a different level of consciousness. The less mature perception of the "believer" and the more mature awakening of the "knower" are both inherent in the nature of reality and the stages of human consciousness. The practice of Sufism is the practice of Islam, but with a recognition of many levels of consciousness. If one is not at least progressing toward that higher consciousness, one is not truly following in the footsteps of Muhammad.

15

The Foundations of Heartfulness

IN RECENT YEARS, the subject of mindfulness has entered into the popular culture. This has been an important step in society's spiritual advancement. While mindfulness has been a common theme in Far Eastern cultures, it represents something almost revolutionary in the West. The idea that there is a state of consciousness other than the "everyday waking state," which most people unconsciously consider "normal," represents a major cultural and spiritual advancement.

In early 1992 when my book *Living Presence: A Sufi Way to Mindfulness and the Essential Self* was published, *presence* was not a common word in the spiritual vocabulary of our culture. In the years since, *presence* has become familiar enough that it is now even being used in advertisements for luxury automobiles or for anything where some intangible quality of excellence is meant.

Presence is more than a synonym for mindfulness, and it has some advantages over the term *mindfulness*. Presence suggests a state that is more than mental, more than focused attention in the present moment. It is a state of comprehensive self-awareness that encompasses body, mind, and heart. It also corresponds with the terminology of Sufism in which various levels of reality are traditionally described as "levels of *presence*." In this tradition, spiritual masters are referred to with the honorific *Hazrat*, meaning "the presence of . . ." The group ceremony of remembrance, zikr, in North Africa is referred to as the Hadrah, "Presence." So this was a very agreeable term to use for that state of consciousness in which the human being is self-aware.

But that is not the end of it, for in the Sufi understanding, the fully human state, though rare in today's world, includes a dimension of heart. And so *heartfulness* is an excellent term for the capacity that arises when we live from what the heart knows.

In *Living Presence*, I described the heart in the following way:

We have subtle subconscious faculties we are not using. Beyond the limited analytical intellect is a vast realm of mind that includes psychic and extrasensory abilities; intuition; wisdom; a sense of unity; aesthetic, qualitative, and creative faculties; and image-forming and symbolic capacities. Though these faculties are many, we give them a single name with some justification, because they are operating best when they are in concert. They comprise an intelligence that is in spontaneous connection to the Universal Intelligence. This total mind we call "heart". . . .

The heart is like an antenna that receives the emanations of subtler levels of reality. The human heart has its proper field of function beyond the limits of the superficial, reactive ego-self. Awakening the heart is an unlimited process of making the mind more sensitive, focused, energized, subtle, and refined, of joining it to its cosmic milieu, the infinity of Love. The heart, in a sense, is spiritualized mind.[1]

In order to establish a strong foundation upon which heartfulness could be understood and practiced, the following could be guiding principles: objective witnessing, practicing patience, clearing the heart, trusting in God, self-less striving, cultivating acceptance, and being pleased with God.

1. *The Objective Witness, ash-Shahid*

Heartfulness begins with a neutral, observing mind. Thoughts, judgments, opinions only obscure the pure state of objective witnessing. Taking the stance of an objective witness allows us to see more impartially. This impartiality is a prerequisite for seeing ourselves and others more accurately, without the distortions of judgment, envy, or fear.

We let go of our judgments of what we see in order to see more. We are not here to judge or blame ourselves or others; that is for the Most Merciful, the Wisest of the Wise. This does not mean that we are blind to right and wrong; but we are not the final judge of others' souls.

Nor does it mean that we give up responsibility for what we see in ourselves; first we must be able to gain objective information about ourselves. We will see ourselves most accurately when we are not afraid of what we might see about ourselves—in other words, when we are impartial. Eventually we may enter a state where conscience and a clear intention can arise in relation to our own weaknesses and distortions and real change can happen.

If we can patiently observe ourselves, simply noticing the stream of judging mind without trying to stop it, we become aware of how much of our lives is spent judging ourselves and others. Our first responsibility is to *see*. If we are too busy judging and reacting, our seeing will be limited, partial, subjective, and distorted.

As we begin to see the extent of our unnecessary thoughts and judgments, we simply allow the mind to become quieter. Witnessing can be supported with conscious awareness of the breath, with or without the repetition of one of the Divine Names. By keeping attention on the breath, the inner chatter will gradually subside. And if at first this quieting seems negligible, if we just trust the process, we discover that something deeper lies beneath all the noise of the mind. The discovery of this deeper knowing, gnosis (*marifah*), is because our own consciousness is sourced in God. To be "near to God" is to be as awake as we can be in all states.

Keep your eye on the Divine Face:
don't stir up dust with discussions and arguments,
you'll just veil the Star with that dust.

149

The witnessing eye is better than the stumbling tongue.
Be silent so that One may speak who calms the dust—
That One whose inmost garment is Divine inspiration.

Mathnawi VI, 2641–47

The Qur'an addresses and consoles the Prophet Muhammad, and indirectly all of us, that not an atom's weight is beyond the awareness of our Divine Sustainer, who is witnessing with us.

And in whatever condition you may find yourself,
whatever discourse of this you may be reciting,
and whatever work you may do—
We² are your witness when you enter upon it:
For not even the weight of an atom on the earth or in heaven
is beyond the awareness of your Sustainer.
And there is neither the least nor the greatest of these things
but are recorded in a clear Book.
Indeed, those near to God—
no fear need they have, and neither shall they grieve:
they who have attained to faith
and have always been conscious of Him.

Surah Yunus 10:61–64

The more the heart is in the state of objective witnessing, the more the heart is unimpeded by judgments, opinions, and preconceptions. The eye of the heart sees like the eye of God.

2. Practice Patience, as-Sabur

True patience comes from the acceptance of the unfolding of time. What benefit can there possibly be in rushing through some moments to get to others? There is a great blessing in simply accepting being here. Our attitude can change from a restless search for content, entertainment, pleasure to the tranquility of acceptance, of knowing and experiencing Divine support. Every moment is the perfect gift of the Divine, manifested for our benefit.

"Tell me truly, how can you know a person's hidden nature?"
"I sit beside him in silence
and make patience a ladder to climb upward:
patience is the key to success.
And if in his presence there should gush from my heart
words from beyond this realm of joy and sorrow,
I know that he has sent it to me from the depths of a soul
illumined like Canopus rising in Yemen."
The speech in my heart comes from that auspicious
    neighborhood.
Surely, there is a window from heart to heart.

Mathnawi VI, 4912–16

The heartful person is aware of this window between hearts and learns to trust it. We are not necessarily looking for some supernatural experience; we are content to experience the spaciousness, this openness of the mind and heart. In this simple openness is the greater possibility to be nourished by the Nourisher, *ar-Rezaq*; to be guided by the Guide, *al-Hadi*; to be forgiven by the One Who Loves to Forgive, *al-Ghafur*; to be illuminated by the Divine Light, *an-Nur*.

We also accept that there will be moments of distraction, difficulty, and challenge, but these are moments in which the soul has the potential to develop and awaken new qualities. Knowing this we can be completely open to each moment, accepting it as it is with gratitude.

The Prophet Muhammad said, "Haste is of the devil." *Surah al-`Asr* 3:1-3 tells us that "everything is in loss," except those who join together for the mutual teaching and encouragement of truth and patience.

And so we return again and again to accepting the moment patiently and contentedly, with the breath of remembrance sustaining us.

And contain yourself in patience by the side of all
who in the morning and at evening invoke their Sustainer,
seeking His countenance, and let not your eyes pass beyond them
in quest of the beauties of this world's life,
and pay no heed to any whose heart
We have rendered heedless of all remembrance of Us
because he had always followed only his own desires,
abandoning all that is good and true.

Surah al-Kahf 18:28

3. Clear the Heart of Idols, La Illaha Il Allah

The testimony *La illaha il Allah* (literally, there is no god but God) is
much more than a statement of belief. It is also a formula for purifying the mind. As we say *La illaha*, we purify the mind and heart by
clearing away our "idols," all that we're inclined to give too much importance to, all that prevents us from seeing things as they really are.
What the Buddhists call "beginner's mind" is in Islamic terms the
mind cleansed of idols.

Know that the life of this world is but a play
and a passing delight, and a beautiful show,
and the cause of your boastful vying with one another,
and of your greed for more and more riches and children.

Surah al-Hadid 57:20

Anyone, to the degree of their enlightenment,
sees as much as they have polished of themselves.
The more they polish, the more they see,
the more visible do the forms become.
If you say purity is by the grace of God,
this success in polishing is also through that Generosity.

That work and prayer is in proportion to the yearning:
people have nothing but what they have striven for.

Mathnawi IV, 2909–13

With a purified heart, we are experiencing life as if from the mind of God. We are seeing through the eyes of God. This consciousness does not judge or blame or evaluate the way our minds habitually tend to do. What we see is often distorted by our desires, fears, and opinions. We fail to notice and be grateful for the gifts of life, for the subtle voice of guidance, because we're so full of inner noise.

Too often we let our thinking and beliefs about what we "know" stop us from seeing things in a new way. If we can learn to cultivate a mind that sustains an objective interest, we will be seeing everything as if for the first time. Being in this empty presence, we are open to real guidance and inspiration that always has a quality of newness, freshness, purity.

No vision can encompass Him,
but He encompasses all human vision:
for He alone is Subtle beyond comprehension, All-Aware.
Means of insight have now come to you
from your Sustainer through this Divine Message.
Whoever, then, chooses to see,
does so for the benefit of his own soul;
and whoever chooses to remain blind,
does so to his own harm.

Surah al-An'am 6:102–4

4. *Trust in the Divine, Tawwakul*

The pure heart is simple-minded. Innocent of any strategies, it implicitly trusts the One who created human nature and educated the character of the prophets and saints. The heart wants to be near the One with whom it is safe from loss or violation.

O heart!
Even if tribulations and misfortunes afflict you,
it is your nature to trust in God,
the One who bestowed your physical eyes and the eye of the heart.
Why, then, are you fixing your eyes somewhere else?

Ghazal 3146

Learning to trust develops out of the mind and heart that has become still and receptive.

Are they, then, not aware that We have set up a sanctuary secure,
while all around them people are being carried away?
Will they, then, place their faith in things false and vain,
and thus deny God's blessing? (*Surah al-'Ankabut* 29:67)

The state of "being carried away" arises out of misplaced faith, desperately seeking for anything to calm our fears, and a mind that is cluttered with inner contradictions. Trust arises out of surrender, the "sanctuary secure," in which we know there is only One to be trusted, the Divine Trustee, *al-Wakil*.

Trust begins with accepting the reality and circumstances of the moment. We cannot truly trust without being fully aware of what is going on.

There are two aspects to trust: the first is that we live in a meaningful and purposeful reality. The circumstances of our lives are continually revealing new aspects of the Divine Mercy and Generosity. Even the difficulties we face can serve to awaken new qualities within our souls. We are all students in a school where the curriculum has been designed in detail for the awakening and development of heart and soul.

The second aspect of trust consists in our ability to be receptive to guidance, to listen to the still inner voice, to witness the signs of God. The more aware we are, the more heartful we are, the more we can trust in our own ability to receive guidance, to see things as they really are, to trust that we are guided from the deeper part of ourselves—the heart that mediates the guidance of Allah.

The more the heart is purified of egoism, the more we can trust and honor our feelings. Trusting in our own authority and intuition is really trusting in the greater intelligence of the Divine. Even if we make mistakes along the way, those mistakes may become blessings, learning experiences. The truly heartful person trusts in the unfolding of each moment.

> Let there be no coercion in faith.
> The right way now stands out from error:
> and so whoever rejects the powers of evil
> and has faith in God has certainly
> taken hold of a reliable support,
> which shall never give way,
> for God is All-Hearing, All-Knowing.
> God is near unto those who have faith, taking them out of deep
>   darkness into the light—whereas near to those who are bent
>   on denying the truth are the powers of evil that take them
> out of the light into darkness deep.
>
> *Surah al-Baqarah 2:25–27*

5. Practice Self-Less Striving, Jihad Al Akbar

The process of spiritual transformation has many levels, each level being a liberation from the tyranny of the false self, from the distortions of vanity and self-interest, from the chains of fear. And each new level brings with it greater knowing, a larger context for our lives, and an increase in our capacity to love.

The reason some of our striving yields poor results is that it originates in the false self, the compulsive ego (*nafs al ammara*). Such striving doesn't have the support of the Divine.

Have you ever considered one
who makes his own desires his deity?
Could you, then, be held responsible for him?
Or do you think that most of them listen and use their reason?
No, they are like cattle—
no, they are even less conscious of the right way!

Surah al-Furqan 25:43

So much of what we do to make ourselves better may arise from a feeling of insufficiency, from negative attitudes about ourselves, from the need to feel superior to others.

The true striving is the striving in God, striving that begins with a clear and noble intention but also recognizes our need for Divine support. Recognizing our need and/or helplessness is the prerequisite for making a sincere call to the Infinite, to the Sustainer of the universes who is all mercy and generosity.

Everything depends on You. Who am I?
Just a mirror in Your hand.
Whatever You reveal, that's what I am;
I'm just a polished mirror.[3]

Ghazal 1397

We do not need to become someone other than who we are. We simply need to become ourselves as we are intended by the Divine.

The best way to achieve our own goals is to back off from egoistic striving and focus instead on carefully seeing and accepting things as they are, moment by moment. With patience and regular practice, movement toward our goals will take place with Divine support and guidance.

But as for those who strive hard in Our cause—
We shall most certainly guide them onto paths that lead unto Us:
for, behold, God is indeed with the doers of good.

Surah al-'Ankabut 29:69

6. Acceptance, Rida

Rida (also spelled *reza*) is to be perfectly content with God's decree. There is nowhere else to begin than with acceptance of where we are, seeing ourselves and our circumstances accurately. We are continually in a state of beginning, seeing what is, embracing the present moment, being willing to see ourselves as we are. In a state of acceptance we are freed of resistance and defensiveness.

The tradition says the spiritual path is like "a bazaar of acceptances." In the past, when some Sufis underwent 1,001 days of training, it was all about acceptance. One thousand and one is the numerological (*abjad*) value of *rida*, acceptance.

Rida is the center of true beginning where infinite Mercy meets our finite self. This encounter between the individual human self and the Divine Mercy is the whole purpose of life on earth. With *rida* the Divine Beauty and Generosity will be apprehended, and the human being will rise to the purpose for which it was created.

> I desire nothing from created beings:
> through contentment there is
> a world within my heart.
>
> *Mathnawi I, 2362*

This Love is longing to be known, to be experienced, to be recognized. The Qur'an describes a state in which we will be "well pleased and pleasing to God" (*radiatan wa mardiyattan*). In other words, your contentment with God becomes God's contentment with you.

> O soul in complete rest and satisfaction!
> Return to your Sustainer well pleased and well pleasing!
> Enter then among my devoted ones!
> Yes, enter my Garden!
>
> *Surah al-Fajr 89:27–30*

When we are content, God is content with us. Earth is mirrored in "heaven," and "heaven" is mirrored on "earth."

One must seek God's contentment, not people's, because contentment, love, and sympathy are "on loan" in people, placed there by God. If He so desires, He can withhold ease and pleasure and then—despite the existence of the means of enjoyment, food, and luxury—everything becomes trial and tribulation.

Signs of the Unseen [Fihi ma fihi], Discourse 63

16

Light upon Light: A Parable

THOSE WHO ARE FAMILIAR WITH RUMI mostly through short ecstatic excerpts know those moments of sudden illumination when the heart hears something it has always known but has never before heard expressed in words. But Rumi is about more than flashes of lightning; even more, he challenges us to live in the continual light of a spiritual sunrise. And for this we need knowledge to guide us, the ability to discern the Real from mere appearances, much polishing of the heart and training of the soul, and the Light of God to augment our own light. Rumi embedded a comprehensive, detailed, and profound methodology in a literary masterpiece of extraordinary beauty that is at the same time a practical and scientific description of the spiritual states leading to human completion.

His passionate concern was to help us fulfill our human destiny and bring our souls to maturity within the conditions of everyday life. Spiritual perception is a theme that appears continually in Rumi's work. The soul is a knowing substance. To understand how the human being's "knowing" can be developed, let us look at an extended passage from Rumi's *Mathnawi*.

You are a Joseph of beauty, and this world is like the well, and the rope to be grasped is patience with the decree of God. Hey, Joseph, the rope is ready! Take it with both your hands. Don't ignore the rope, it has gotten late. Praise be to God that the rope dangles here, that grace and mercy have been woven together, so that you may see the world of the new spirit, an invisible world that has been made manifest.

Mathnawi II, 1276–79

The prophet Joseph, who is mentioned in both the Old Testament and the Qur'an, is thought to be one of the handsomest men who ever lived. Out of jealousy for their father's devoted love for him, his brothers tied him up and suspended him upside down in a well. That well, however, became Joseph's place of spiritual retreat where he deepened his experience and understanding of Divine mysteries—this is how God cares for his sincere friends.

All human beings are potentially the heirs of the prophets. There is a beautiful Joseph inside each of us. This world sometimes seems like the well Joseph was imprisoned in, yet we are offered a rope woven from the strands of grace and mercy that not only allows us to escape from the well but to enter a "world of the new spirit, an invisible world that has been made manifest." This is the promise of spiritual transformation: a new capacity for perception.

This world without real existence has appeared as if it were the true reality, while the world of true reality has become very hidden. The wind plays with the dust, waving a veil, a false display. What seems to be so very busy is, in truth, just idleness, a mere surface phenomenon. That which is hidden is the core and the source. The dust is only a tool in the hand of the wind, while the wind is of the highest Source.

Mathnawi II, 1280–83

Here is a fundamental lesson in metaphysics. We live in a world of appearances, and we are deceived that this world is the ultimate reality. Physical existence occupies all our attention, and we are heedless of what lies beyond physical appearances. On the surface, things seem to be happening, but the real cause and purpose of outward events is hidden from view. The world of merely physical phenomena is just dust in the wind.

The eye of dust gazes only on the dust, but another eye is needed to see the wind. One horse knows another horse, just as a rider knows what pertains to another rider. The perception of the five senses is the horse, the Light of God is the rider: without a rider, the horse itself is useless.

Mathnawi II, 1284–86

The physical senses, the eyes of dust, are only good for physical perception, but another kind of "seeing" is possible. The animal self, the horse, needs to be trained by a higher consciousness, or rider. Light must be added to light; self-awareness must be added to mere sensory awareness. The "rider," conscious presence, must be awakened.

So train the horse: take its bad habits and transform them into grace and skill fit for a King. The horse's eye must find the way from the eye of the King; without the King's eye its situation is grim. If you call the horse to anything but grass and pasture, it says, "No, why should I?"

Mathnawi II, 1287–89

The horse's habits are the result of its natural inclinations. It is content just to graze. The horse does not reach its full potential until it has been trained. Some will want to train the horse for war; some will want to train the horse to be a beast of burden; some will train the horse to race around the track. But the King wants to train the horse to be a royal steed, fit to carry the King in beauty and dignity.[1]

Light upon the Senses

Not until the Light of God mounts on the senses does the soul yearn for God. Does a riderless horse know the signs on the road? A King is needed to know the King's road. Accustom yourself to senses encompassed by Light; that Light is the senses' best companion. The

*Light of God augments sense perception; this is the meaning of
Light upon light.*

Mathnawi II, 1290–93

In the Qur'an, God is described as "Light upon light." Here Rumi
equates this Light with a quality of consciousness that can accom-
pany and augment the physical senses. This new level of consciousness allows the horse and rider to see the signs of the road and so to
find their way to the King.

> The light of the senses is attracted to the world; the Light of God
> elevates the whole being. The senses perceive a limited world: the
> Light of God is an Ocean, compared to which the senses are just
> a drop of dew. But the Light that governs the senses is proven by
> positive actions and words.

Mathnawi II, 1294–96

One kind of light is for the physical world; the other kind of
light transforms us. One kind of light is a drop; the other Light is
an Ocean. But this new quality of Being is not merely some mental
phenomenon, nor merely a state of awareness without fruit; it transforms character. It has an impact on our actions and words. It has
moral import.

> The sensuous light, which is coarse and heavy, is hidden in the
> empty black pupils of the eyes. Since you do not even see sensory
> things by means of physical substance, how will you see the light
> of a spiritual being by means of your eyes? If the light of sensuous
> things depends on this intangibility, why shouldn't the subtle ra-
> diance be even more hidden?

Mathnawi II, 1297–99

Now comes a very subtle point. Even the physical eye perceives
by means of its own emptiness. The pupil of the eye is a nonphysical

opening that converts sense impressions to another frequency of the electromagnetic spectrum that is then interpreted by the brain as the tangible, physical world. If the so-called physical world is perceived by means of this subtlety of perception, how much subtler is the perception of the spiritual world that is yet more hidden?

The Hand Is Hidden While the Pen Writes

> *This world, like chaff in the wind of the Unseen, has taken help-lessness as its only practice. By the dispensation of the Unseen it becomes high or low, whole or broken, to the right or to the left, now thorns, now roses. See how the Hand is hidden while the pen writes; the horse careening while the Rider is out of sight; the arrow flying while the Bow is unseen; countless souls manifest while the Soul of souls is hidden. Don't break the arrow; it belongs to the King. It is not shot at random; it is from One who knows how to hit the target. God said, "You did not throw when you threw": the Divine action precedes our acts.*
>
> *Mathnawi II, 1300–1306*

The Qur'an says, "There is no power nor agency but with God." All of physical existence is merely the effect, not the cause of anything. The real Cause and its purposes are hidden to ordinary perception. The Qur'anic verse "You did not throw . . . but God threw" (*Surah al-Anfal* 8:17) is said to refer to a moment when the Prophet Muhammad was in battle with a small band of companions. They were on the verge of defeat when he picked up a handful of pebbles and flung them at the attacking army. It turned the battle and resulted in victory. This verse has been interpreted by the mystics as suggesting that the actions of those who are merged with the Divine become a direct manifestation of the Divine Power.

Break your own anger, don't break the arrow. The eye of your anger sees milk as blood. Give the arrow a kiss and bring it to the

King—the arrow stained with your own blood. What can be seen is helpless, confined, and feeble; while that which is unseen has strength and authority. We are the hunted; who set the trap? We are the ball in the game of polo; who wields the mallet? He tears and He sews: where is the Tailor? He blows, He ignites; where is the Kindler? One hour He makes the true saint an infidel; then He makes the atheist into an ascetic.

Mathnawi II, 1307–12

The arrow is a symbol of any circumstance that life hurls at us. To respond with resentment or resistance is to break the arrow, but if we take the arrow, even and especially when it has been stained with our own blood, and return it with a kiss to the King, we demonstrate our trust and submission. That mysterious power can and does transform thorns to roses. But it is up to us to dismantle our anger and resentment rather than rail against the circumstances we face. We must become masters of our own inner lives rather than be mastered by circumstances, but this is only possible with humble, tender trust. We must kiss the blood-stained arrow.

For even the sincere one may be entrapped until he is completely rid of self, because, while still on the Way, the brigands are numberless. If he has not become a clear mirror, he is only an attainer; if he has not caught the bird, he is still a hunter. But when the attainer has become the attained, he is delivered. He has reached the station of security and attained the goal. No mirror ever became iron again; no bread ever became wheat. No ripened grape ever became sour fruit. Mature yourself and be safe from a change for the worse. Become the Light.

Mathnawi II, 1313–19

Until we are completely transformed, "completely rid of self," we are not out of danger. What does it mean to be "rid of self"?

To be a sincere seeker (*mukhlis*) is to strive toward complete sincerity (*mukhlas*). The former sincerity is merely descriptive; the latter signifies one who has completely become what the word describes. For Rumi, spirituality is about the total moral and perceptual transformation that is possible when one has been matured by Light upon light.

To say it another way: the fulfillment of our human destiny is ultimately through the development of spiritual perception. This science is called *irfan*, signifying the realization through knowing. Nothing less can satisfy the human heart.

17

Personal Sovereignty

Claiming Our Divine Inheritance

Perhaps you have known people who thought that spirituality was all about losing themselves. Perhaps they heard the Sufi concept of *fana*, often translated as the "annihilation of self," and attempted what was neither desirable nor possible. Why do we bring up the idea of "personal sovereignty" at this time and oppose it to this notion of selflessness?

What do we mean by personal sovereignty and why is it important? How can the development of the self be reconciled with the spiritual life? To understand this development, we need to consider both personal sovereignty and Divine Sovereignty and their relationship to each other.

Sovereignty over oneself could be thought of as the ability to consciously choose the good, to follow one's highest purpose, to live an authentic life free from the coercion of outer or inner forces. The outer forces could be the prejudices and negative influences of our culture, community, or family. The inner forces could be our selfishness, fears, or need for attention and approval. In fact, all unhealthy emotions arising from a wounded or traumatized personality will impede a person's ability to act as a sovereign individual. It is a rare human being who has not been damaged by life, whose natural innocence has not suffered from the unconscious behavior of fellow human beings.

The quest for personal sovereignty is the subject and substance of many dramatic tales in which an individual faces challenges to living an authentic life. Everyone is potentially on this heroic journey, facing inner and outer obstacles that must be met with courage and wisdom.

> Have the aspiration of a falcon
> and the pride of a leopard.
> At the time of the hunt be graceful,
> and be victorious at times of war.
> Don't get too involved
> with the nightingale and the peacock.
> One is all words and the other all colors.
>
> Quatrain 1078[1]

Not only must the hero overcome the obstacles on the path but they also must prevail without undo harm to others. If on this heroic journey of life we leave behind a trail of destruction and grievance, we adulterate our personal sovereignty; our personal sovereignty cannot exist on a foundation of injuries and wrongs. The hero's journey must eventually include the righting of past wrongs, the healing of karmic wounds.

Sovereignty over oneself means to be able to stand before God with humility and sincerity, recognizing, with our limited strength and wisdom, that we have done our best.

Sometimes in Sufism the concept of fana is misunderstood to mean the annihilation of individual will and merging with and surrender to Divine Will. But character and virtue are meaningless unless we have chosen them through our own free will.

Personal sovereignty is the claiming of the creative power of free will, our Divine inheritance. As human beings, we have the potential to develop will, *the capacity of conscious choice in the moment.*

The power of conscious choice
is your profit-earning capital.
Pay attention!
Watch over that moment of power!
The human being rides on the steed of
"We have honored the children of Adam" (*Surah al-Isra* 17:70).
The reins of free will are in the hands of intelligence.

Mathnawi III, 3299–300

Personal sovereignty matures with the discovery of our own inner purpose. Every human being has enormous potential, no matter how buried it may be. We carry within us the potential to awaken and manifest certain spiritual attributes, and we have been given self-awareness with which to know ourselves objectively and recognize our unique possibilities. Personal sovereignty begins with the recognition of the freedom of the soul to activate the latent capacities of the soul.

O pure people who wander the world,
amazed at the idols you see,
what you are searching for out there,
if you look within, you yourself are it.[2]

Quatrain 549

The Forces That Shape Our Sense of "Reality"

The spiritual crisis of our times is the loss of personal sovereignty due to the pervasive influence of a false reality sustained by social media, news media, mass entertainment, and even more ominous technologies of mind control. Humanity is more and more governed by narratives that shape our sense of who we are, what is possible for us, what threatens us, what we should look and act like, what we should believe, and ultimately what the purpose of our lives might be. In the modern secular world, where freedom supposedly reigns, most people live with the illusion that they have a reasonable grasp of reality and can make reasonable choices based on their sense of reality.

But what forces are shaping our sense of reality today? We are facing unprecedented distortions of reality through pervasive communication technologies owned and operated by global elites and the corporations and governments that serve them. Whether power ultimately resides with a hidden cabal or a more random selection of forces greedy for power and wealth, we still face the pervasive influence of messaging that appeals to our fears and lowest desires.

In past centuries the consensus reality was shaped by traditions that changed only slowly and were, to some extent, the result of inherited wisdom and accumulated experience. Whatever the shortcomings of these traditional frameworks, they were relatively stable. In the past century, however, it has become possible to radically alter the collective sense of reality. Traditional and indigenous forms of wisdom could be replaced by ideologies and commercial forces. Cultures that were once the result of humanity's best insights and practical wisdom can now be transformed in short order and even degraded by an appeal to our baser instincts. Whoever controls the media, whether out in the open or behind the scenes, controls the narratives that shape our sense of reality.

We can be manipulated through our fears for survival, instinctual desires like sexual gratification and the search for pleasure, narcissistic needs for acceptance and approval, and all the ways we judge and blame other human beings and groups for our own unhappiness and lack of fulfillment.

How are we going to effectively do the spiritual work when we fear the terrorists lurking among us, or believe that the purpose of life is to acquire the latest gadget or make ourselves sexually attractive, or when we judge others who are different from ourselves and fail to recognize our common humanity?

Whether the dominant reality is engineered along the lines of an Orwellian scenario or a merely chaotic and incoherent barrage of commercial messaging, our spiritual well-being is threatened, consciousness is assaulted, and our hearts need healthy sustenance. Junk foods, junk entertainment and media, unsustainable lifestyles, and inordinate desires compromise and corrupt our souls.

Since the power of mind control comes from its ability to dictate a governing narrative through which we experience the world, spirituality today needs to be the rewriting of that narrative based on the deepest truths of spiritual realization. However much the dominant narrative may have limited our sense of human possibilities, rewriting the narrative is still possible, and rewrite we must. This is an essential step in reclaiming our personal sovereignty.

As difficult as it may be to forge an independent narrative of human life, extended virtual communities or small groups sharing their lives, if informed by wisdom traditions such as Sufism, can preserve and sustain this quest for a truly human life.

But personal, individual sovereignty is only one side of the equation. Individual sovereignty prepares us for recognizing our dependence on Divine Sovereignty, where true agency resides. Our capacity for individual sovereignty depends on the degree of our connection with Divine Being. It is that connection that frees us from whatever depletes the soul.

No Prayer Is Complete without Presence

O God, there are so many traps, so many baits,
and we are like hungry, greedy birds.

Every moment we're caught in some new snare,
even when we might become a falcon or bird of the heavens.[3]
O You who are without need, each moment You free us,
and then again we fall into another trap!

We put grain into our barn, and then lose it.
Why don't we consider that this loss
comes from the gnawing of mice?
These little mice have devastated our barn.

O soul, first stop the mischief of the mice;
then work to gather the grain.
Hear a saying of the Master of Masters:
"No prayer is complete without presence."[4]

If there is no thievish mouse in our barn,
where is the harvest of these forty years of devotion?
Why doesn't the sincerity of each day accumulate,
bit by bit, here in this barn?

Mathnawi I, 373–84

We're like birds that take the bait again and again, each time losing our freedom, our sovereignty over ourselves. Every grain of spiritual attainment we hope to store up is depleted by the mice in our barn. Only a prayer offered with presence can summon the Divine support we need. Only then can we become a viable container for Spirit.

It is in the maturity of the sovereign individual that the purpose of existence is fulfilled: to recognize and know that we are loved, that we are born from love, and that we fulfill our human destiny by responding to the Love that created us. The purpose of individual sovereignty is to awaken to the creative power of the Divine Love within ourselves.

18

Coherence of the Soul

Have you seen the one who chooses his own passions as his god?

Qur'an, *Surah al-Furqan* 25:43

What Is Coherence and How Is It Possible?

A coherent sentence is clear and comprehensible. A coherent argument is lucid and rational. Coherent light is the very definition of a laser. So what is a coherent soul?

If we look at our own experience, we may recognize states in which we are unfocused, distracted, confused. We may also recognize that parts of our life do not quite fit together. One part is frugal, another part is wasteful. Some parts are organized, but some are chaotic. One part is kind, another part can suddenly be mean. We lack coherence. We are made up of various needs and desires, various impulses and constraints, various subpersonalities that conflict with one another.

This is not unusual, and to some extent it is the human situation. Nevertheless, we could benefit from more coherence in ourselves and our lives. We might also recognize that there are some exceptional people who are more often in a state of coherence. We might also have experienced moments when we were much more coherent, when our thoughts, feelings, and actions were more in a state of flow.

The origin of our incoherence is the instability of the ego. By its very nature the ego does not have a center. Even when it may seem to have a dominant tendency, "a one-track mind," it is still subject to contradictions, negative reactions, and uncontrollable impulses. The ego, unless aligned with Spirit, is inherently incoherent.

Sometimes egoism can be so strong that it tries to assert itself as if it were a god, as if it could bend reality to its will. It thus creates a distortion within the field[1] that produces disharmony and suffering. It does this in small and large ways, in trivial matters and sometimes on a tragic scale.

There may be many ways for human beings to become more coherent, but fundamentally they all have to do with a strong, magnetic heart in resonance with Spirit, capable of bringing the disparate parts of ourselves into a harmonious order. As much as we might try to attain single-pointedness, a focused attention, our efforts will be weak unless we ourselves are in a state of harmony or coherence.

A strong heart, a magnetic center, depends on our intimate connection with the Transcendent. Coherence is an aspect of the Divine Reality. As we regularly affirm in our tradition, "Everything in existence is the manifestation of the one Source of life and being."

Personal coherence is the embodiment of Divine Coherence. It is a sense of selfhood deeply rooted in a trust of that Divine Coherence. The Source of Life is continually manifesting both beneficence and purpose. The coherent soul trusts in the providential nature of life's unfolding. Suffering and loss, pleasure and joy, everything can ultimately be for the benefit of our souls if we are conscious and grateful.

And so coherence of the soul comes from trust in the Source of Life.

On Commitment and Coherence

One of the lessons that a true spiritual path may teach is the value and possibility of commitment. The essence of it is this: *Commit to the Way and the universe will rise up to support you.* But before such a commitment is possible—a commitment requiring sincerity, knowledge, personal sovereignty, and faith—we would do well to consider some realistic first steps that might be more within the range of possibility for us.

On the Sufi way, intention is something that we hope to practice many times a day. Before an act of worship, we express the intention inwardly or outwardly: "I intend to perform a certain number of prostrations of such and such prayer." We consciously remind ourselves that we are intending exactly what we are doing rather than heeding our ego's whims and desires.

One result of unconsciously following our ego's inclinations is a dispersal that leads to indecision and incoherence. Sometimes we may deceive ourselves with the idea that we are "going with the flow," when actually we are simply going with what seems the path of least resistance. In such a state we do not see that we are merely reacting to circumstances, governed by our likes and dislikes, forgetful of our higher intentions. In reality we may be enslaved to momentary happenings and the ego's ever-changing whims.

In the end, so much depends on our capacity for will, which we can define as "conscious choice." This is one of the most fundamental attributes of a human being, yet will as conscious choice remains undeveloped and unrealized in many human beings. Not until presence is sufficiently developed is a healthy will possible.

Human will is a gift of the Divine, given to us that we might use it wisely. "God's will" is not necessarily something separate from this. To develop and use our will in the service of love and truth is a sacred responsibility and a very high human attainment. Perhaps the only state higher than this is to be so in alignment with the highest Truth that it seems we have no will at all. We can imagine some human beings whose hearts are so pure, who are so free of selfish egoism, that they feel no choice but to do what is right and good and true. In our tradition it's said that when the human heart is sufficiently purified, the All-Compassionate sits on the throne of the heart and guides it directly.

Returning to the more realistic level at which we live, our lives would benefit from more conscious choice, from decisions intentionally made and brought to completion as much as possible. Every decision we make but carelessly leave incomplete drains us of will. We need to continually exercise our will, building the muscle of conscious choice rather than living a life of heedless dispersion.

Purifying the heart and awakening will are major steps in developing personal coherence. There is coherence in having a sense of purpose in our lives and choosing our activities: how we use our attention, what we give our time to, and what we value, in light of this fundamental sense of purpose. It is one thing to have a broad vision and an open mind; it is quite another thing to scatter ourselves carelessly. One respected teacher summarized a lifetime of spiritual teaching with the following advice:

- Decide what you want to do.
- Start doing it.
- Keep up your spirits.
- Don't make it too important.

Of course, this simple advice presumes a great deal of wisdom as its foundation.

The ultimate coherence, however, is total reliance on God. In the moment-by-moment unfolding of the pattern of our lives, we trust that this life is an educational program designed especially for us by an Infinite Intelligence and Compassion. This trust is not passivity, fatalism, or a superficial going with the flow. Rather, this is the highest development of will. It is a state in which we consciously watch the unfolding of time and circumstance, always saying "thank You," trusting, giving our consent to every moment, knowing that we are blessed and guided by an Infinite Intelligence and Love and that we have nothing to fear. As it is said in the tradition, make all your cares into a single care and God will see to all your cares.

The Incoherence of Postmodern Culture

Postmodern culture is a profoundly incoherent phenomenon. While, on the one hand, we are more aware of the interdependence of humanity and our environment, the exploitation of people and the environment continues. And though there are glimmerings of a spiritual awakening, the postmodern mentality is predominantly one of hyper-materialism.

What we have instead is an emerging global culture without a center, fundamentally cynical toward all propositions of truth. In the postmodern world there is no objective truth, only personal truths, and these are believed to be based in prejudices of class, ethnicity, religious affiliation, and other forms of conditioning.

We are faced with the collapse of a coherent sense of truth, the loss of an objective metaphysical perspective, and a cynicism about the best of traditional values that were in harmony with such a metaphysical perspective. Inevitably, we ourselves are affected by the cultural and spiritual incoherence around us.

One of the more common forms of suffering that we witness around us and within us is the difficulty of attaining coherent wholeness. An example of this might be: "I want this, but I also want that, and I can't decide between them, because I'm not sure what I really want." Another example might be: "I decide to do one thing, and then change my mind, and then I'm not sure if I should have continued what I was doing in the first place, or maybe I should be doing something altogether different." This kind of dispersion affects not only decision-making but also our relationships, our beliefs, our work, and in fact every aspect of our lives.

Whatever the dominant mentality may be, we have the possibility and the responsibility to create coherent communities of intention, spiritual microclimates, in which souls may develop and flourish.

Establishing Coherence in Ourselves

The first step in this process is to retrieve our attention that has been scattered across the myriad of preoccupations both in the outer world and our inner world. Retrieving our attention is gathering ourselves to a single point of Being from which we can objectively witness every moment, every condition of life with trust and gratitude.

Postmodernism may have originated in the necessary "deconstruction"—the effort to break free of all false perspectives, social masks, superficial identities—but it has left people without the recognition of any fundamental being or soul.

In this milieu, nothing is taken seriously, no fundamental truth is affirmed—only the relativity of all cultural postures. This postmodern culture tends toward a cynical commentary on all perspectives.

I recently watched a documentary in which two Hollywood actors toured a traditional Mediterranean village known for its healthy lifestyle and the exceptional longevity of its people. These two men were continually assuming the identities of various other actors in a parade of humorous impersonations, a superfluous overlay in stark contrast to the simple and authentic lives that were being observed. Establishing personal authenticity and coherence in today's postmodern milieu is a countercultural movement.

The work of attaining personal coherence recognizes the superficiality of many social identities, lifestyles, cultural fads, and political ideologies. The work of spiritual coherence rests upon a firm foundation of true humanness arising within the core of our being.

The heart is our connection to the Infinite. But we need a purified heart in order to develop a "coherence of being" so that when we become still and look within our deeper self, we find there what we're looking for. We find our connection to Infinite Being. We can know Infinite Being beyond this material existence. We can come to know that what is truly real is not all this "stuff" that changes and comes and goes.

Do not invoke any "deity" but God.
Worship nothing except Hu (the Divine Presence).
Everything is perishing except that Face,
with Whom all ordainment resides
and to Whom you will return.

Surah al-Qaṣaṣ 28:88

Everything else is perishing. All this is perishing. What is Most Real? It is something beyond circumstances. It is something beyond conditions. We've been given a heart that can know and "see" that Face. The heart is for that purpose alone. To experience something that is beyond circumstances that is infinitely compassionate. Every human being has the capacity to know this. Moreover every "problem" of life is eased with this awareness of Infinite Compassionate Being.

All of our troubles, worries, and fears are due to simply a disconnect from Infinite Being Itself. "And the Garden shall be brought near for the God-conscious" (*Surah Qaf* 50:33). For whom? For those who witness the circumstances and events of their lives from the perspective of the Transcendent. Those who turn toward the Real and preserve this connection.

So we have this situation where we have been losing this capacity to have a heart that sees, that can perceive the spiritual nature of existence. We have externalized our concerns. We're living "out there" and living in our reactions to what's "out there." We have been neglecting to cultivate this essential connection with Infinite Being that comes when we open up to the stillness and the peace that is the root of the root of the root of the self. All of our problems and worries are from the self that has become disconnected from Being.

Fear and Hopelessness

One of the characteristics of this era of acceleration and intensification is that people are living in fear. Many of these fears are imaginary, a kind of social hypnosis that comes through the media. We're conditioned to fear. The media broadcasts fear to gain and hold people's attention. Governments use fear to manipulate and control their citizens.

People of faith, the "God-conscious," have much less fear. I once saw a news report where a reporter went up to a man during the bombing of Baghdad, asking, "Aren't you afraid? Aren't you afraid?" And this faithful Muslim said, "No, why should I be afraid? It's 'written' when I will die. Either I will die or I won't die. Why should I be afraid of that? If I fear that, I will die a thousand deaths before I die." Well, it can be that way for all of us.

Another characteristic of our time is a sense of hopelessness that compounds that fear, a hopelessness from seeing all the problems of the world, including unending distractions and dysfunctional politics, with nobody seeming to know how to change all this. So people rightfully feel a sense of hopelessness as well as fear. This is simply the reality of many people's lives. And no matter how deep our spiritual practice, no one is completely immune from the woes and worries of humankind because we participate in a common psychic atmosphere.

Forms of Coherence

Negative states such as fear, resentment, arrogance, and selfishness represent a disordering of the field of coherence. These negative states lead to disharmony in our relationships and, finally, leave us at war with ourselves.

A coherent human being reflects a strength of being, a radiation of blessing, a power of intention. An incoherent human being lives in a state of self-contradiction, doubt, second-guessing, hypocrisy, duplicity, insecurity.

A spiritual path offers us individual practices and collective ceremonies of coherence, but all of them have this in common: awakening a point of observation within ourselves, allowing us to view our incoherence, and eventually restoring a state of relative peace and coherence.

In *salaat*, the ritual prayer, we gather all our human faculties into a single, coherent act of reverence. In Sema we whirl around a single inner axis, emptying ourselves of everything but pure presence while connecting to the lineage that exists beyond time. In *muraqaba*, watchful meditation, we become a single-pointed awareness. In adab, spiritual courtesy, we govern the incoherent impulses of our egoism and cultivate conscious harmony. In *halvet*, solitary retreat, coherence is strengthened through being alone for a number of days in reflective silence.

The ritual prayer can potentially unify the individual with the ultimate coherence. Likewise, zikr is a powerful practice for unifying all our faculties, capacities, and attributes through a vibrational coherence.

Coherence in a group can be increased by the state of coherence of each individual, by participating in coherent activities (salaat, zikr, music, ceremony), especially those activities that are harmonized by movement, rhythm, tone, and pitch.

I have loved the classical music culture that developed over centuries in the Mevlevi lodges, a music that developed within a community continually focused on the sacred. The music expresses that state, and it can be felt by the listener.

The quality and soul of a society or community reveals itself in the music it creates. Mevlevi Dedes composed many classical compositions in different modes (*makams*), expressing nuances of the soul: aspiration, courage, devotion, ecstasy, humility, tenderness, and joy. Communities that share a musical culture that reflects the richness of the soul will have pleasure, vigor, and well-being through the spiritual qualities of such music.

Coherence is a musical phenomenon, and this is why music has been essential to our Sufi path. Coherence within a community can facilitate the experience of Spirit. Like an arrangement of antennae or transceivers in a phased array, our vibration can be strengthened far beyond the capacity of any individual. Through this common vibration we are given a taste of the Divine that would be very rarely experienced alone.

And yet a coherent community is almost always the result of some alignment with one or more human beings who have reached a deep state of coherence themselves.[2] Such people are like the magnetic heart of the community, radiating blessing and coherence. In our contemporary, supposedly egalitarian society, we are suspicious of hierarchies, but this is not a hierarchy of privilege or power but rather of service and selflessness. It is from such a community that we may get a "taste" of what spiritual maturity is, and that taste can be transformative.

> Is there any one person who is worth a thousand others?
> The saint. Actually, that servant of the Most High
> equals a hundred generations.
> The great rivers kneel before the jug
> that has a channel to the sea, especially this Sea of Reality.
>
> *Mathnawi* VI, 22–29

The human being who has that "channel to the Sea" makes it easier for those who are seeking this connection to become more coherent, more harmonious, both in themselves and in relation to others.

> The hearty unripe grapes, capable of ripening,
> as last become one in heart
> by the breath of the masters of heart.
> They grow rapidly to grapehood,
> shedding duality and hatred and strife.
> Then in maturity, they rend their skins,
> till they become one: unity is the proper attribute
> for one who is one with others.
>
> *Mathnawi* II, 3723–25

The Beauty and Power of Coherence

In a state of incoherence, the parts of ourselves are not unified but in a state of inner conflict and contradiction. Rumi describes[3] how humanity is oppressed by four heart-oppressing tendencies personified by a duck, a peacock, a rooster, and a crow. Collectively they are the destroyers of our good sense. Just as the prophet Abraham was advised to sacrifice these four birds, we are advised to cut off the heads of these birds in ourselves and to "revive them in another form in which they can do no harm."

The duck represents greed, its bill always rummaging in the mud or dirt, like a thief in the night who turns the house upside down, hastily stuffing into its sack everything it can grab. It lives in fear that it will be caught in the act or that there is not enough time, and so its life is full of worry and stress.

Rumi contrasts this with the person of faith "who conducts his foray in a calm, leisurely manner." He has no fear of "missing his portion" because he trusts in the King's power and justice.

Then there is the rooster whose preoccupation is lust. Rumi tells how the Devil (Iblis) was begging God for something with which he could effectively tempt men. God brought forth luxurious riches and sumptuous foods, and Iblis was not impressed. Then he offered intoxicants and licentious music, and Iblis faintly smiled. But finally God brought forth a temptation of physical beauty, the fleeting beauty of flesh that could prevail over reason and self-restraint, and it was then that Iblis snapped his fingers and said, "Now I've got just what I want."

And there is the crow with its cawing, its noisy cries. The crow is demanding of God a long life, but it is a tasteless life estranged from the Divine Presence. It wants to lengthen its life all the way to the Resurrection purely for the purpose of eating sh . . .

Next we come to the two-faced peacock, entirely absorbed in vanity, name, and fame, hoping to catch the attention and admiration of people. What will this predator achieve with its narcissism?

Its life passes quickly, and rather than catching anything of value, it is caught in the trap of its own "beautiful appearance." The ambition of the peacock is like the hunt for the wild pig—extremely fatiguing and yet in the end you cannot eat even a morsel of what you caught. The greed of the duck for grubs is trivial, but the greed of the peacock for eminence is vast. The sins of the duck and rooster, gluttony and lust, are small sins compared to the sins of the vainglorious peacock—pride, vanity, and arrogance. The peacock is unconsciously competing with God Himself, and who can redeem a sin of such proportions? If the peacock could gain true wisdom it would realize that it allowed its own feathers to become an enemy of its essence.

Rumi, in his inimitable wisdom, says, the only thing worth pursuing is Love, and yet Love is not caught by any trap of yours. Don't be a predator; become God's prey.

> Love is whispering into my ear,
> "To be a prey is better than to be a hunter.
> Make yourself My fool:
> renounce the high estate of the sun and become a speck!
> Come dwell at My door and be homeless:
> don't pretend to be a candle, be a moth,
> so that you may taste the savor of life
> and contemplate the sovereignty hidden in servanthood."

Mathnawi V, 411–14

The Coherence of Commitment

One of the lessons that a sincere spirituality may teach is the value and possibility of commitment. Existence can be a mirror in which we see ourselves. If we are half-hearted, vacillating, doubting, existence is filled with uncertainties, contradictions, randomness. On the other hand, for the person who commits to the Way, the universe will rise up to support them.

But before such a commitment is possible—a commitment requiring sincerity, knowledge, and faith—we would do well to consider some realistic steps that might be more within the range of possibility for us.

On the Sufi way, intention is something that is practiced many times a day. If we're going to worship, we express the intention inwardly or outwardly: "I intend to perform X number of prostrations of the such-and-such prayer." If it is a fasting day, I say, "I intend to fast today by the grace of God." We consciously remind ourselves that we are intending exactly what we are doing, rather than just going along with the flow, by which I mean following the path of least resistance.

We have a special word that signifies going with the flow when the flow is truly flowing: *zuhurat*. It means being open to synchronicity, spontaneity, and miraculous manifestations. Sufis know the state very well; more and more of life may take on this quality but not to the exclusion of those practices that we intentionally perform, practices that include an awareness of time, presence of heart, and a deep penetration of consciousness. As with so many things in the spiritual life, the relationship between intention and spontaneity is not either-or but both-and, quite consciously.

All spiritual work depends on intention—intention being an orientation of the soul and attention. Intention is the very essence of the soul, a capacity to be developed by the spiritual seeker. However, we should not misunderstand intention as being merely fulfilling the wishes of the self. There are higher and lower intentions, a hierarchy of intentions.

Sufi practice contributes to the development of intentionality in innumerable ways. We learn to make more and more of our daily acts intentional—our ablutions, our prayers—and ideally every action begins with intention. The simplest form of this is to say *"Bismillah"* before beginning any activity, meaning "We do this in the name of God."

This world is a sorcerer,
and we are the merchants who buy
yards of measured moonbeams.
When it takes the money of our life,
our purse is emptied, and we are left without linen.
You must recite, Say, I take refuge,
crying "O You who are One, come,
save me from those who cast knotted spells."
    (*Surah al-Falaq* 113:1, 4)
But invoke Him with the tongue of deeds as well,
for the tongue of mere words is weak.

Mathnawi V, 1044

A Vast, Transcendent, and Tender Truth

The Prophet invited certain people to make a commitment to the
Way by saying,

This is my way: I call on Allah with conscious insight (*basirah*),
I and whoever follows me—*subhanallah*—and I am not of those
    who worship other than God.

Surah Yusuf 12:108

Surely, those who promise allegiance unto you,
promise allegiance only to Allah.
The hand of Allah is above their hands.
So whoever breaks a commitment,
breaks it only to his or her own hurt;
whereas whoever remains true to what is pledged to God,
upon them God will bestow an immense reward.

Surah Fatih 48:10

COHERENCE OF THE SOUL

These are also the words spoken during initiation (*bayat*) into Rumi's path. The commitment to the Way is based on that deep seeing. It's about awakening perception.

Such a commitment arises not primarily from an experience of a vast, transcendent, and abstract Truth but even more from an encounter with an intensely intimate and tender Truth.

Again and again Rumi reveals the awesome truth that the Divine is seeking us, even more than we are seeking the Divine. It is through the human heart that this generosity and beauty become known. For some it is the most complete expression of mercy that they have ever encountered.

That mercy is the way of Abraham, Jesus, and Muhammad. In the Sufi understanding, Islam is not just a sect, not just a religion called Islam, but the primordial religion of humanity, the root of all religions.

Rumi is always showing us the dynamic relationship between the individual human soul and this awesome overpowering mercy that exists to transform us. Rumi often gives that mercy a voice:

> I've come to drag you by the ear
> to make you selfless and crazy,
> To take you inside your heart and soul.
> I've come to you, My lovely rose,
> to be with you like spring,
> to hold you beside Me
> and to pour some wine for you.
> I've come to reveal your beauty,
> and just as the vows of lovers promise,
> to take you above the sky.
> Who is this rose but you yourself?
> The power to command, sovereignty, is with you.
> Even if no one else knows you,
> once you are Me, I recognize you.

You are My Spirit and My Soul.
It is you who recites the Fatiha for Me.
So become the Fatiha, now!
And I will call you in my heart.
You are my catch even though
you try to run from My trap!
Come, return to the trap again
or I will drive you toward it.
There's no escape. . . .
Why are you running around Me?
I will rip right through you!
Or embrace your wounds and charge forward
with the Shield of Holy Courage!
Don't listen to anyone else!
I will give you all the arrows you need.
From the dust of the threshold
to the perfection of being human
there are a thousand abodes.
From city to city, moment by moment,
I will show you every step of the way.
Say nothing! Don't take the lid off the pot.
Simmer well and be patient while I cook you.
Don't you know that in essence
you are a fearless lion,
veiled by the body of a deer?
And I will take that veil away.[4]

So, Rumi is the fulfillment of the revelation that came so clearly with Muhammad and Jesus and Solomon and David, may they be blessed, and countless prophets and true friends of God, known and unknown. Rumi is of the same spiritual DNA. This is not a different message. This is not something other than the root of the root of the root of religion.

Now, inspired by those words comes the hope and the reassurance that you are meant to be a spiritual wayfarer. It's not so impossible. It's difficult but it may be easy compared to all the other choices. It's easier than being tyrannized by your own *ego*. It's a path of discipline, but it is also the way of happiness. It is also the way of turning the inevitable suffering and the inevitable pain of life into a maturity of the soul.

In many cases it's with our pain that we begin. If we didn't have some pain, we wouldn't search. We wouldn't yearn. We might be comfortable somewhere not thinking about these things, but our pain has brought us here, our yearning has brought us here. Ultimately, love has brought us here.

But let Rumi explain this as only he can:

> There are some of God's servants who approach God by way of the Qur'an. There are others, very rare, who come from God only to find the Qur'an here and realize that it is God who has sent it. "We have surely sent it down; and We will certainly preserve the same" (*Surah al-Ḥijr* 15:9). The commentators say this is about the Qur'an. This is all well and good, but there is another meaning here, namely, "We have placed in you a substance, a desire to seek, a yearning, of which We are the keeper. We will not suffer it to be wasted and will bring it to fruition."

> *Signs of the Unseen [Fihi ma fihi]*, Discourse 26

The Coherence of Love

So, the substance of yearning has been placed in the very core of our being, and this substance is guarded and destined to be realized. The vast Coherence of Being is seeking to reintegrate each separate self into this Coherence through the power of love.

Truly spiritual love—that is, love with no object—is the most coherent phenomenon in existence. Love is the ultimate state of coherence because it unifies the individual with the Ultimate Reality of the field of existence. Practically speaking, love is a magnetism of the heart that engenders a coherent ordering of all our human faculties. When we are aligned with love, we experience coherence, and we bring coherence into the world.

People can become addicted to "falling in love" because they taste even momentarily that pull into a focused coherence that seems to bring them a depth of feeling and purpose. When a human being "falls in love with Love," that personal coherence is increased but without dependence on a personal object of love, an earthly beloved.

The spiritually coherent human being is like a polished mirror, simply reflecting what is before it. When such a person meets some-one who is full of personal anger, rage, or judgment, the more mature one remains coherent and centered, grounded in unconditional love, and the other may see themselves in the mirror of the spiritually coherent one.

Suleyman Dede,[5] who guided us for the last six years of his life, was such a mirror for us. He once said, "In order to become human, we need to always be within the Divine Presence—to be aware of God, to hold Him in our hearts. When a human being performs zikr, their spirit—their heart starts to open. Their intelligence becomes more refined and more expansive. Their bodies become healthier. A beautiful condition comes about—similar to the one that is brought about by good music. The whole being opens up like a flower, and the secrets—the things you couldn't understand or know about be-fore—begin to be revealed to you. This is why it's necessary to make zikr. For human beings, it's a very good thing."[6]

O You who have transmuted one clod of earth into gold,
and another into the Father of humankind,
Your generous work is the transmutation of essences;
my work is mostly forgetfulness and mistakes.
Transmute my mistakes and forgetfulness into knowledge:

With my imperfect nature, turn me into patience and
    forbearance.

Mathnawi V, 780–82

God, your Sustainer, is the Real. Other than the Real
What is there but error? How have you been misled?
Thus the word of your Sustainer is proved true
against those who do harm, they are without faith . . .
Of these that you take as your "gods,"
are there any that can guide to the truth?
Say, "It is God alone who guides to the truth . . ."
But most of them follow only conjecture, and conjecture
is of no value with regard to the truth.

Surah Yunus 10:32–36

May we return to the deep coherence within, dive beneath the
opinionated mind, the unstable emotions, and know the Ocean beneath the waves.

19

Higher-Order Reality

EVERY HUMAN SOUL is in the course of life acquiring certain experiences. Does it matter that we acquire experience? Does this serve any purpose? If we go through life relatively unconscious, numb, unappreciative, ungrateful, and absorbed in our petty desires, what might we be forfeiting? What if souls have been sent into the world in order to share in ontological ecstasy and love and to be eternally enriched?

If the soul-essence can simultaneously receive sensory impressions while being aware of its own essence, then a bridge, a connection, a communion is possible, a meeting between the Divine and the human. A channel is opened between different levels of existence, and the soul is imbued with spiritual qualities and meaning. There is a way of meeting experience that allows our soul-essence to be inscribed, imprinted with the impressions received by life in a way that is elucidating for the soul.

Poets and artists to some degree cultivate this quality of experience. Others may live only at the level of thing-ness in a relatively lifeless world, driven by their egos' desires to somehow satisfy insatiable desires that material existence in itself cannot satisfy. Some poets, artists, mystics, and lovers consciously experience the momentousness of the moment, the presence of eternity within time, the radiance of love behind all phenomena.

The soul that begins to live in a state of remembrance, in conscious relationship with the holy Presence, that soul-essence is impressed and inscribed by its experiences, gradually acquiring something like flavor and fragrance, overtones, hues of that Presence. In other words, the soul is affected and changed qualitatively.

It learns from every experience, not only the so-called good experiences. It will learn from its "mistakes" as much as from doing things "right." It will learn as much from its sorrows as from its joys. This is the real meaning of Divine Mercy (*Rahmet*). When the soul is conscious, humble, and grateful, every condition of life teaches us about life itself. Such a soul is at least partially aware that all of life is emanating from a higher-order reality.

The soul sometimes senses that higher reality as the master Truth, the essential reality that unifies all experience. The more the soul has experiences of this kind, the more magnetic and powerful it becomes. This magnetic power brings coherence within ourselves. This coherence is the power of the soul functioning in harmony with a higher reality. Yes, it is becoming powerful, but it is not the power of personal self-will apart from Divine Will.

Self-will is the inverted aspect of our free will. We are free to turn away from the Real, to disconnect from the Divine Presence, but the one who takes the path of self-will gets compromised or even ambushed by negative (shaytanic[1]) forces.

In contrast, the soul-essence that lives with humbleness, gratitude, and love is enveloped by mercy and ecstasy and develops into a coherent radiant body of light. The soul-essence that has gained some independence from material and egoistic attachments can survive the dissolution of the physical being that has been its temporary vehicle. According to some views, whoever does not attain this coherence and radiance will, at best, cling like a famished ghost in the regions of its fleeting desires and attachments and eventually disintegrate. Nothing, however, is completely lost in this universe; everything serves some purpose. Everything is food or compost for something else, and that is an aspect of cosmic beneficence.

The Sufi path is designed to help the soul-essence develop its coherence and participate in the ecstasy of the Divine. It is a joyous process because even the smallest details of life are experienced as a gift. No suffering goes to waste; no joy is taken for granted. The illusions of the separate ego are gradually dismantled and the soul realizes its essential nature. Through opening to a network of interdependent loving relationships, the false self is more and more erased. This is how the soul is cooked, made flavorful, and qualitatively transformed.

Human Nature and the Divine Names

The completion and fulfillment of our human nature is through the realization and actualization of the Divine Names inherent in our nature. The complete human being is the one who has realized the Divine Names.

These Names enumerated in the Qur'an are fractals of a qualitative nature. They reveal a qualitative dimension of existence. Everything in existence is the manifestation of a single Source of life and being. Everything unfolds from the Divine Source through laws, proportions, and what today we understand to be fractals. Fractals are self-similar reproductions of an innate pattern that follow mathematical ratios, and especially the ratio of phi, or 1.618. The Divine Names mentioned in the Qur'an are not mathematical fractals but fractals of the all-encompassing Divine Beneficence.

The ultimate nature of the Divine is described as abundant, merciful love (rahmah).

My Mercy encompasses all things.

Surah al-A'raf 7:156

Each of the Divine Names is not a self-subsisting entity but an attribute of God. The Name and the Named are One.

The foremost manifestation of this Divine Love for us in the human realm is the sending of prophets and messengers, who are the recipients of direct inspiration and guidance from Universal Intellect.

We sent you (O Muhammad), only as a mercy to the worlds.

Surah al-Anbiya' 21:107

Certain Divine Names

Allah is *al-Latif*, the Subtle, the force that maintains the creation by the subtlest and gentlest means. The human being who becomes cognizant of this, who perceives the subtle grace of God in supporting the creation, has awakened to the attribute of al-Latif.

Allah is *al-'Adl*, the Just, and only someone with the most comprehensive wisdom can know the extent of God's justice in detail. Nevertheless, through our experience of mercy and compassion we may learn to trust that Divine Reality is ultimately just even if we cannot perceive it from the segmented view of our own consciousness. As a matter of principle, we learn to aspire to justice. We learn to govern our emotions and desires so as not to be unjust, for "The word of your Rabb, your Sustainer, is fulfilled in justice" (*Surah al-An'am* 6:115).

Allah is *al-Fattah*, the Opener through which whatever has been closed may be opened—opening hearts, opening secrets, opening mysteries, opening the Way. Al-Fattah is the key to everything that is locked up. Al-Fattah is the means to any true "victory," which is above all an opening.

Allah is *al-Jabbar*, the Compeller whose will and influence governs all of creation. Yet His compelling is not necessarily through force or violence but through the power to shape and restore form and natural order, the way a broken bone is mended by the body's own resources. Muhammad was al-Jabbar in the way he became an example for humankind. He was a cause, not an effect. Through his inspired example, a noble way of life was exemplified.

Al-Khaliq, al-Bari, al-Musawwir: These three Names occur in proximity to each other at the end of *Surah Hashr*. It is significant that three words, all signifying aspects of creativity, should be grouped together in this important passage that contains the greatest density of Divine Names in the Qur'an.

Al-Khaliq is the One who creates out of nothing. Al-Bari is the One who creates the exquisite structure and order of creation. Al-Musawwir is the One who molds, shapes, and forms.

The creativity of the Divine Names is a source of continual wonderment and gratitude. If we accept the responsibility of being fully human, the Divine Creativity will flow through us.

The Role of Creativity in the Spiritual Life

The central significance of creating and creation is mentioned in the very first revelation of the Qur'an, *Surah al-'Alaq*:

> Recite, in the name of your Sustainer who created,
> created the human being from a germ-cell.
> Truly, your Lord is the Most Generous,
> Who taught with the Pen,
> taught the human being what it did not know.
>
> *Surah al-'Alaq* 96:1–5

The Sustainer (*Rabb*) is the one who taught with the cosmic Pen. The point of the pen and its ink are here on earth, while the Pen itself extends through all levels of existence and is ultimately in the invisible "hand of God." This Pen connects all levels of reality and is the axis of Being.

God is al-Khaliq, the Creator, and in fact the only true Creator. While in one instance, Jesus is said to have "created" a bird "as a sign from God," the revelation frequently points out that nothing and no one, except for Allah, really creates anything out of nothing. In the Qur'an, only God is described as "Creator."

Scientists now recognize that life began on Earth not from a random lightning bolt igniting some cosmic soup but rather through a process of oily bubbles taking shape that led to the emergence of organisms. In other words, through a process of containment, complexity unfolded in an intelligent way. Life developed within form. There was an encounter between the latent material of life and some invisible form-giving energy.

In the natural world, life-forms are continually manifesting new responses to environmental conditions. Discoveries in biology, for instance, reveal the extraordinary capacity of life to be creative. Mechanistic notions of biological processes are being replaced by something called complexity theory that suggests the spontaneous emergence of new patterns of order. Particularly at moments of systemic instability, new forms of order are seen to emerge. This is the power of Divine Creativity at work.

From the Islamic perspective, the human being is created in the "noblest proportions" and is the "representative caretaker" of the Divine. This corresponds to the idea that the human being is made "in the image of God." So, the human being is to some extent the carrier of the creative power of the Absolute, which is grounded in a timeless, witnessing presence that engages with the ever-changing conditions of life. Through the encounter of these two realities—the eternal reality of presence and the diversity of life in all its manifestations—truly creative action becomes possible. Thus, the human being potentially shares in the Divine creative power.

Creativity in the Human Being

To develop ourselves along the lines for which we were created is to integrate the necessary and unavoidable work of being alive as a human being with the conscious, joyful creativity that comes from the union of opposites. We are continually faced with two drives: one is toward the sensuous world of our mortal selves; the other is toward an ideal, rational, structure-creating capacity, an ordering power that comes from "above."

If we completely succumb to the sensuous, we descend into hedonism or wanton decadence. If we are too dominated by the structuring drive, we become puritanical and oppressive. We see this tyrannical domination of the life force in most fundamentalisms.

The result is an oppressive moralizing on matters of sexuality and gender, an antagonism to the free movement of energy in dance and music, and a dismissal of the role of the arts in educating human sensibilities. Religion, if untempered by the humble details of our humanity, will encroach upon the sacred ground of spontaneity and creativity and eventually oppress the life force itself.

The optimal state is one in which natural desire is guided and given form by transcendent Intellect, while that Intellect is also tempered and grounded in all the beauty of nature and humanness. The natural world is evidence of the Divine Creativity, and human beings can experience the wholeness and completeness that is the marriage of heaven and earth.

Rumi tells the story of a person who had mysteriously fallen ill and was visited by Muhammad. It's a very long meditation on the challenge of living with a "carnal soul"—the dangers of being dominated by bodily impulses, and how even after wayfaring for many years one may be held captive by bodily desires. After some questioning the Prophet ascertained that the sick man had prayed to be punished for his sins in this life rather than in the afterlife. Caught in the loop of self-hatred and blame, the ailing man had committed the metaphysical error of giving precedence to a punitive concept of the Divine. The Prophet urges him to abandon inviting God's punishment and to invite Divine blessing instead. Rumi puts it this way, drawing on the Qur'an, *Surah al-Baqarah*, verse 201:

> The Prophet said to the sick man:
> "Pray like this: Rabbina (Our Lord),
> grant us what is most beautiful in this world,
> and in the world to come,
> and save us from the agony of the Fire."
> Make the Way for us as subtly beautiful as a garden.
> You, O Noble One, are our aim and our blessed Gift.
>
> *Mathnawi* II, 2551–53

The spirit of Sufism embraces the particular, the sensual, the musical, and the poetic as expressions of the Transcendent. Great souls like Rumi remind us from where our hearts receive their nourishment. Lovers are those who are aware they live in a universe of creative energy.

THE BEAUTY

For lovers, the only lecturer
is the beauty of the Beloved:
their only book and lecture and lesson is the Face.
Outwardly they are silent,
but their penetrating remembrance rises
to the high throne of their Friend.
Their only lesson
is enthusiasm, whirling, and
not the precise points of law.

Mathnawi III, 3847–49

Principles of Creativity

Human beings can receive knowledge in unexpected ways from Infinite Intelligence, but it doesn't happen purely by chance. The characteristics of a creative life begin with a state of mental openness but also include some form of focus, sustained attention, letting go into the subconscious mind, and finally a breakthrough. Creativity comes when we are capable of living in the medium of our creativity.

We can identify some basic principles for living in the creative medium:

- To seek all the knowledge relevant to our discipline.
- To ask: What do I really understand of the problem or question?
- To rigorously ask the question: Am I going to take this task seriously or not?

- To have faith that there is a solution to the problem or question, or situation, whether we can see it or not.
- To let ourselves become empty, to exhaust ourselves if necessary, so that something new can enter. At this stage it is necessary not to accept only the expedient or easy solution or answer but to have the discernment to wait for a treasure to be revealed.

People who have experienced major creative breakthroughs have almost always occupied themselves with a burning question to the point of exhaustion, then let go, and finally experienced a breakthrough, an inspiration, or a symbolic vision. Examples include Samuel Taylor Coleridge's *Rime of the Ancient Mariner*, Rainer Maria Rilke's *Duino Elegies*, Lawrence Bragg's work with crystallography, and August Kekulé's dream of what we now know as the hydrocarbon ring.

When faced with a compelling question in our lives, all of us search for an answer. Creativity arises in response to such a question—which may not necessarily fall within the domain of the arts or our everyday work. When faced with extraordinary difficulty or grief, for example, creativity can transform despair, or even rage, into beauty. How often do we live in the intensity of a question as opposed to living in a state of habit and numbness?

If we wish to amplify the creativity in our lives, we need some form to contain the latent energies of creativity, otherwise they will simply disperse, leak away, and expend themselves in trivial pursuits. Each of us has a definite amount of life energy, which can be decreased or increased to some extent but needs, most of all, to be given a container. The form-giving capacity is essential to the creative process.

We may define creativity as the ability to make something new, useful, or beautiful by combining given ideas or materials in unexpected ways. These could be forms of relationship, community, or education. They could be songs, poems, or other works of art.

By assuming our creative role as human beings in cooperation with the Divine Creativity, we become people who live with a sense of beauty and create expressions of beauty. We can avoid the slavery to sensuality, on the one hand, and the tyrannical oppression of the life force on the other. Eternity is in love with the ripened fruits of time. Heaven and earth are meant to balance each other. With this balance of the sensuous and the transcendent, with feeling and reason, with passion and detachment, with natural desire and intellect, the drudgery of life can become creative play, and we can experience the breakthrough of spiritual wisdom and guidance in facing life's conditions.

> If you are so in love with art;
> why not dip yourself like a paintbrush in the paint?
>
> Ghazal 2134

The work, which must also be a form of play, is the process of transforming the blind necessity of labor in the physical realm into a free and joyful choice. It is in the joyful choice to undertake work in a creative way that leads to true freedom and beauty. It is in this way that our life itself becomes a work of art and the human being develops into a "beautiful soul." Or as Rumi expresses it,

DIVING FOR PEARLS

Someone said that we have come to know each and every condition of mankind. Not an iota of man's condition and nature or his hot and cold humors has escaped us; yet it has not been ascertained what part of him will abide forever.

If that could be known merely by words, then such effort and exertion would not be necessary and no one would have to go to such pain or toil. For example, someone comes to the seashore. Seeing nothing but turbulent water, crocodiles, and fish, he says, "Where are the pearls? Perhaps there are no pearls." How is one to obtain a pearl merely by looking at the sea? Even if one measures out the sea cup by cup a hundred times over, the pearls will not be found. One must be a diver in order to discover the pearls; and not every diver will find them, only a fortunate, skillful one.

The sciences and crafts are like measuring the sea in cupfuls; the way to finding pearls is something else. Many a person is adorned with every accomplishment and possessed of wealth and beauty but has nothing of this intrinsic meaning in him; and many a person is a wreck on the outside, with no fairness of feature, elegance or eloquence, but within is found the intrinsic meaning that abides forever. It is that which ennobles and distinguishes humanity.

Signs of the Unseen [Fihi ma fihi], Discourse 50

20

Life in the World

THE JOURNEY OF THE SOUL begins with an ineffable longing; develops on the basis of diligent, practical work; and finally realizes its maturity in a humility free from vanity and self-assertion. To attain a healthy, balanced self, we embrace the simple principle: "Claim nothing for oneself; let the Divine do." This principle is a way of purifying the heart, refining intention, and inviting the Transcendent into our lives. It is not a merely passive state. The ability to consistently apply this principle results from a very high development of presence and will. To move beyond the promptings of the false self, to enter into the free-flowing state of spiritual intelligence, is the work of a lifetime.

Perhaps what surprised me most in my early days on the path was meeting people who lived very practical lives—whether as engineers, teachers, cooks, musicians, artists, doctors, and even military officers—yet sustained a course of constant intellectual development and a pattern of practice involving regular prayer, fasting, and continual remembrance.

As a contemplative and lover of Truth, I trust that my life's integrity is possible through a living relationship with the Transcendent. It is through this relationship that it is possible to fulfill our human destiny to be a bridge between heaven and earth.

Contemplation and Inspired Action

Contemplation is a term we use for an inner process that directs awareness toward the Transcendent. It is not, as some might imagine, a sort of dreaminess divorced from everyday reality, much less a withdrawal from responsibility. While it might be possible for a human being to train attention on some abstract plane or become lost in subjective fantasy, this is not what we mean by contemplation. True contemplatives know that it is possible to cultivate a relationship with a transcendent dimension, an overflowing source of grace and intelligence that shifts our experience of life.

This transcendent Source has been described with a verbal noun, *Being*, because what is contemplated is not a *thing* but *an eternal verb*. In contemplation it is possible to come into relationship with a spiritual power, a primordial imperative, the command to "Be," and be profoundly changed by it.

The very yearning to contemplate tells us something about ourselves: that we have an inherent capacity to reflect upon our origin and purpose. In other words, it is part of our nature to contemplate, and what we contemplate is something intimately resonant with ourselves.

If an apple could contemplate, it would contemplate the apple seed, and from there glimpse the wholeness of apple-ness. In contemplating its seed, it would glimpse its origin and its mature fruition.

What of the human seed? What is the life-unfolding principle behind a human life? Is it the genetic code? Or is it something more than our biological inheritance? The contemplative knows, both from personal experience and from the age-old metaphysics of contemplation, that there is a light within us, a consciousness more fundamental than our actions, emotions, or thoughts; more fundamental even than what we might call our personal self. It is in some way more fundamental, more primary, than that manifestation that we identify as our own personality or character. This is what is meant by the Mysterion. It is a pole of our being that is transpersonal even while it includes qualities that are profoundly personal.

This Mysterion is the point of contact with Spirit, which virtually every traditional sacred culture identifies with a secret within the breath. It is as if the Divine Breath has breathed something into us. Just as the apple seed carries the "spirit" of the apple, there is a human essence that carries the spirit of our humanness.

If we analyze the process of contemplation that leads to the realization of the spirit within, this process might be divided into two stages: emptying and receiving; or to put it another way, clearing and perceiving.

In the stage of emptying, we still the body, quiet the thinking mind, and disengage from everyday desires and emotions. This emptying is not to permanently abandon emotion, the thinking mind, and the body but to reconnect with something deeper. By connecting with this deeper essential self, we also reduce the influence of our egoism. By focusing on our deepest center, these other aspects of our being will naturally become more still, quiet, coherent, and wise.

Wisdom emerges when we neutralize the false self, that generator of distortions, compulsions, and fears. When we remove some of the physical, mental, and emotional veils that obscure perception, the essential self can express itself with less interference.

I remember my amazement the first time I watched ski jumping when I lived in Vermont. How could somebody ski down that ramp and, leaning forward, soar through space so fearlessly? The training of a ski jumper is partly physical but even more the attainment of an inner state that allows the jumper to let go of fear and soar. A ski jumper trains the mind as much as the body in order to achieve a single graceful act of courage.

What lengths we human beings will go to in order to experience that freedom and perfection! Contemplation is like ski jumping but even more inspiring, because its effects resonate through every detail of our lives. Contemplation helps us to develop a capacity to release ourselves into life with trust.

Contemplation leads us to a perfect balance of being, action, and love. It helps us to see more clearly the struggle between the relatively superficial, unreal parts of ourselves and the deeper intelligence of the essential self.

If our action does not originate in a deep quality of Being, it lacks the coherence and wisdom necessary to bring wholeness and reconciliation into the world.

If our love does not originate in a deep quality of Being, it is a shallow, grasping, emotional, or worse yet, merely sentimental love. Such a love can easily be discouraged, or it can even turn into its opposite. It can be weakened and distorted by the false self's grasping, neediness, and insecurities. But love that originates in Being is a love that is energized and sustained by the unconditional Infinite Love.

The Meaning and Purpose of Our Actions

So, in order to understand the relationship between contemplation and action, we must put these themes in their proper perspective. What kind of action does contemplation inspire, support, inform, and guide? What is the purpose of contemplation and, perhaps even more importantly, *what is the meaning and purpose of our actions here on earth?* What do they serve?

This question is especially relevant at this time when the moral foundations and implications of our society and economy must be called into question. Are we offering spiritual guidance that will enable people to be more adjusted and comfortable in an unjust and insane system? Are we offering consolation when we should be inspiring questioning and heroic engagement?

While religion and spirituality are deeply concerned with the condition of humanity, earthly life is not an end in itself; this worldly life is not the ultimate value. There may even be some values worth sacrificing our lives for.

From the vantage point of the eternal soul, life on earth is an opportunity to develop the eternal qualities of the soul. The fables of heavenly reward hint at the ontological reality that all human intentions, choices, and sacrifices have a corresponding reality in the dimension of Spirit. The values of self-less generosity, integrity, self-sacrifice, and unconditional love have a spiritual reality that ennobles the trials, tests, and sorrows of life. This is at the heart of all sacred traditions. Sacrifice is one of the most compelling of spiritual themes.

It continues in the Islamic tradition where the word *shahid*, used for someone who sacrifices their life for a cause, actually means "witness." In this case, a "witness" is someone who has sacrificed for a true and noble cause. There are things worse than death: injustice, oppression, moral corruption, and especially the tyranny over hearts and minds. Some people put their lives on the line to stand up for truth, justice, and unconditional love.

The Heroism of Abdul Qadir al-Jazairi

Of those who have put their lives on the line, some of the greatest of these have been Sufis, and one of the greatest of these was Abdul Qadir al-Jazairi, who led a rebellion of North African tribes against overwhelming odds, challenging the French, who were at that time the most powerful military force in Europe. Though his campaign ended in defeat and surrender, it inspired the world. He and his forces fought courageously, but when it was clear that there was no chance of winning, he negotiated an honorable surrender. Nevertheless, he was betrayed by the French and imprisoned for some years.

Afterward, Abdul Qadir settled in Damascus and befriended Sir Richard and Isabel Burton. His knowledge of Sufism and skill with languages earned the Burtons' respect and friendship. Isabel wrote of him,

> He dresses purely in white . . . enveloped in the usual snowy burnous . . . if you see him on horseback without knowing him to be Abd el Kadir, you would single him out . . . he has the seat of a gentleman and a soldier. His mind is as beautiful as his face; he is every inch a Sultan.[1]

Abdul Qadir's feats of heroism would not end in Algeria, however, because while in Damascus he boldly intervened in a conflict between the Druze and the Maronite Christians. The Druze had attacked the Christian quarter, killing over three thousand people. Abdul Qadir previously warned the French consul as well as the Council of Damascus that violence was threatening; when it finally came to pass, he sheltered large numbers of Christians, including the heads of several foreign consulates as well as religious groups such as the Sisters of Mercy, in the safety of his own home. Abdul Qadir sent his eldest sons into the streets to offer sanctuary to any Christians under threat.

> We were in consternation, all of us quite convinced that our last hour had arrived . . . . In that expectation of death, in those indescribable moments of anguish, heaven, however, sent us a savior! Abd el-Kader appeared, surrounded by his Algerians, around forty of them. He was on horseback and without arms: his handsome figure calm and imposing made a strange contrast with the noise and disorder that reigned everywhere.[2]

Abdul Qadir was in the lineage of Muhyiddin ibn al-Arabi, one of the greatest Sufi metaphysicians. That he was a man of action is only made more remarkable by the fact that he was also a gnostic (*arif*) who comprehended the stations leading to spiritual realization.

> The first "station of separation" corresponds to the state of the ordinary man who perceives the universe as distinct from God. Starting from here, the initiatic itinerary leads the being first to extinction in the divine Unity, which abolishes all perception of created things. But spiritual realization, if it is complete, arrives afterwards at the "second station of separation" where the being perceives simultaneously the one in the multiple and the multiple in the one.[3]

This great revolutionary hero who made extraordinary sacrifices and accomplished great feats of self-less heroism was also capable of understanding that the station of Unity, oneness with God, was not the ultimate spiritual attainment but that the polarity between Lord and servant, Creator and creature, can be lived as the ultimate state of human maturity, as witnessed by the example of the Prophet Muhammad.

> But, in conformity to His wisdom it was right that afterward the Prophet should be sent back from the vision of pure Unity and that he should return . . . toward the separative vision. For He created man and djinn only that they should worship Him and know Him—and, if they remained at the degree of pure Unity, there would be none to worship Him. In this separative vision, the Worshipped and the worshipper, the Lord and the servant, the Creator and the creature are again perceived.[4]

The human being who has experienced this degree of intimacy with the Divine is the one who can devote themselves heroically to the welfare of humanity. Such is the ideal of Sufism.

The disease we are suffering from in the world today is a collective toxic *egosis*. We dwell in the parts of the mind that are individual and separate, analytical and critical, relativistic and cynical. We have not been taught to connect the intellect, or conscious mind, to the vast Oneness that unifies us all. Our societies rationalize selfishness, privilege, and dominance over nature and over people who are economically weaker.

To the extent that we as seekers have cultivated a certain quality of attention within ourselves and cleared our hearts to be spiritually receptive, we are the recipients of an overflowing grace, guidance, and love. Does that give us the right to be content with our own spiritual states? Or does the knowledge and experience of spiritual reality compel us to a spiritual activism, to being the very voice of transcendent unity, to turn up the light of the Spirit in this darkened world?

Even if Abdul Qadir al-Jazairi was betrayed by the French government and suffered humiliating imprisonment, his struggle was not in vain. As with the Christ, worldly triumph was not necessary for his purpose to be fulfilled.

Some illuminated beings will be drawn to heroic actions, great tasks, and whether their sacrifices lead to triumph or defeat, something in the domain of the invisible is accomplished, completed.

For others, there may be a gentler, no less heroic path, one that is potentially available to those of us who are not called to make such a mark in history. Each of us must find the noblest elements within our own tradition that can contribute to resolving the arguments and conflicts in the world.

A story about `Ali that has been handed down is an example of matchless nobility and self-less striving. While in battle, `Ali was about to thrust the coup de grâce when the young warrior spit in his face. `Ali, recognizing his own anger, threw down his sword and refused to kill his opponent in that state of anger. These are the words Rumi has `Ali speak at the climax of book one of the *Mathnawi*:

> For God's sake, for Reality
> whose slave I am, I wield this sword.
> The body does not command me,
> nor does the lion of craving
> overcome the lion of God.
> Like a sword wielded by the sun,
> I embody these words in war:
> Thou didst not throw when thou threwest.[5]
> I've dropped the baggage of self.
> That which is not God is nothing.
> God is the sun, and I am a shadow.
> Jeweled with the pearls of Union,
> my sword brings life in battle, not death.

Blood will not dull my shining sword;
nor will the wind blow my sky away.
I am not chaff but a mountain of patience.
What fierce wind could lift a mountain?
What the wind blows away is trash,
and winds blow from every side—
the winds of anger, lust, and greed
carry away those who do not keep
the times of prayer. I am a mountain,
and my being is His building.
If I am tossed like a straw,
it is His wind that moves me.
Only His wind stirs my desires.
My Commander is love of the One.
Anger is a king over kings,
but anger, once bridled, may serve.
A gentle sword struck the neck of anger.
God's anger came on like mercy.
My roof in ruins; I drown in light.
Though called "the father of dust,"
I have grown like a garden.
And so I must put down my sword,
that my name might be He loves for God's sake,
that my desire may be He hates for God's sake,
that my generosity might be He gives for God's sake.
My stinginess is for God, as are my gifts.
I belong to God, not to anyone else;
and what I do is not a show,
not imagined, not thought up, but seen.
Set free from effort and searching,
I have tied my sleeve to the cuff of God—
if I am flying, I see where I fly;
if I am whirling, I know the axis on which I turn;

if I am dragging a burden, I know to where.
I am the moon, and the sun is in front of me.
I cannot tell the people more than this.
Can the river contain the Sea?

Mathnawi I, 3787–810

`Ali is human, not superhuman. He has normal human reac-
tions, but he also has the presence to rise above those reactions and
remember his purpose. He cannot allow himself to give in to hatred.
The result of `Ali's forbearance is that the heart of his opponent was
touched by `Ali's state. He sees this transformation in the young war-
rior and utters these words:

Since I am free, how should anger bind me?
Nothing is here but Divine Qualities. Come in!
Come in, for the grace of God has made you free,
because His mercy had the precedence over His wrath.
Come in now, for you have escaped from danger:
you were a stone; the Elixir has made you a jewel.
You have been delivered from the thorn thicket of kufr:
blossom like a rose in the cypress garden of Hu.
You are I and I am you, I am happy with you:
you are `Ali—how should I kill `Ali?
You have committed a sin better than any act of piety;
you have traversed heaven in a single moment.

Mathnawi I, 3825–30

Hatred is not halal for the spiritual warrior. We must even be
able to forgive those who have projected their own violence upon
us, because reacting with hatred only proves them right and perpetuates further cycles of violence. This is true on the level of societies
and even more true on the level of individual, personal life. If we can
forgive everyone everything, the grace of the Divine will always be

there to meet us. One never knows how the Divine will bring forth the truth in another human being.

If we could trust in that grace, the Divine Intelligence will more and more provide us with something to do or say that would cause the other to lay down their weapon, withdraw their projection of evil, and experience the possibility of peace. Somewhere in the world a child, a woman or man, a family will be safe and able to live in peace.

We pray that the next generation will give birth to a language for the peace beyond war, as all of humankind goes beyond these jealousies, arguments, and conflicts. Let us strive for a unity that honors diversity and difference; unity does not require uniformity. Let us recognize that unity is the original design feature of existence.

Those who profess a commitment to spirituality carry a great responsibility. They are answerable to the biggest questions of human life and existence. What is of ultimate value? What is the purpose and end of life? What is the nature of being human? What is the Mysterion within all life to be honored and served?

21

Oneness on the World Stage

Seeing the Divine in All

In considering how the world works and what a program for a more harmonious Oneness might entail, what would a spiritual solution be? Operating within a realistic view of the world, is there any strategy for how to attain a conscious transformation of societies?

The political obstacles are great; to describe them in detail is far beyond the scope of this book. Amid what seems like a cacophony of voices, arbitrary violence, staggering hypocrisies, we have to keep our hearts intact. To redeem such a many-layered system of ignorance and corruption by focusing on the symptoms would do little to disempower the primary force causing those symptoms. And strategies aimed at the many individual political, social, academic, corporate, and institutional structures that make up the dominant system would not change the vibrational nature of their activities. The system is locked within a frequency range that resists meaningful transformation.

But there is no force stronger than spiritual realization. And there is reason to be hopeful that enough people will awaken from the narrowly egoic station and graduate to the level of true individuality—an individuality in resonance with a higher-order reality, a connection to the sacred.

The egoic condition of humanity is one in which people are afraid of giving up a position they have adopted as a defense, afraid that something will be imposed on them, taken from them, or that they will be harmed or violated by another.

The tenderest souls fear that if they open to love, their love will be betrayed. The psychopaths, on the other hand, whose souls have withered almost to nothing, totally lacking in empathy, act upon others without regard for the suffering they cause.

The common response is to first look out for oneself and one's family, and if that involves competition with others in a zero-sum game, so be it.

The "lovers," in contrast, are less dominated by self-interest and competition. They keep faith and do the work, and existence mysteriously supports them. Because they are aware of the reciprocal, interdependent nature of reality, they benefit from a collaboration with the Unseen.

The lover is always asking, "What shall we do with the Oneness?" The unrealized human being is responding with various defenses: "You're not of my race, my ethnicity, my culture. I don't like your name for God. You're wearing strange clothes. Don't get so close. What do you want from me?" Or, " Look how special I am. Pay attention to me. Why aren't you behaving as I want you to?"

What shall we do with the Oneness? The dimension of ourselves that "knows" is informed and guided by the awakened heart and by higher consciousness. It is an intelligence beyond the limited self. It is a territory of the mind that is vast and the servant of cosmic love. The awakened heart can gain some perspective on the false self and moderate its demands. It stands on a spiritual promontory that can transcend the drama; it can laugh and let go.

It's all well and good to say we will love humanity, but the awakened heart forges the bonds of oneness one person at a time. Every time we can see another as our self, every time we see others' needs as important as our own, we are bringing heaven down to earth.

And if the awakened heart must confront the depths of the principalities of evil, it will be given the wisdom and the courage required, for there is no circumstance that does not ultimately serve the unfolding and manifestation of Truth.

The Practice of Oneness

Oneness (*Tawhid*) has been one of the central concepts of the Way, even if its true essence has often been like a buried treasure waiting to be discovered. *Tawhid* has implications and results far beyond what most imagine.

From the beginning, Islamic civilization has been governed by the values of Tawhid. It expanded in a way unprecedented in human history through this integrating power. Compared to other civilizations, and no civilization is without contradictions, Islamic civilization sought to include and incorporate "others" under the principles of compassion, dignity, and justice.

One Friday I was at a local mosque for the weekly congregational prayer. A guest imam was giving a rousing sermon, and we all know what a disturbing time Muslims are passing through. The gist of the sermon was that Islamophobia has always been present, that every prophet who came to the world faced challenges, and that Muslims should realize they are being tested. Furthermore, we should not let the extremists define our religion for us. The imam was addressing a community made up almost entirely of immigrants when he said, "We came to this country because of its laws, and we are not the enemy of this country, or of any country." These people have had to encounter bias, fear, and hatred because of their Muslim identity, especially as a result of so much misunderstanding and distortion following 9/11. And yet that identity was the best of what they were. The imam ended by saying, "Dear brothers and sisters, they do not hate us—they do not know us."

I happily stand with them and support them, and I stand as well with another community that I call "the custodians of consciousness."

The Custodians of Consciousness

There are Sufis, and mystics of all traditions, who have been among the "custodians of consciousness"—those who maintain and benefit from an awareness of higher levels of reality. They can integrate the personal dimension of consciousness with the imaginal and the unitive levels of consciousness. They have perceived that everything in existence reflects consciousness, intelligence, and eternal life. As custodians of consciousness. they move through life with humility, patience, intuitive awareness, and love.

The custodians of consciousness bear a special responsibility. There has always been a certain portion of humanity whose level of consciousness is relatively free of the biases, superstitions, jealousies, and self-righteousness that enslave so much of humanity. These custodians are the mystics, the gnostics, the peacemakers, the wise, whose hearts and minds are less contaminated with the toxins of egoism. If the custodians of consciousness increase in number, humanity might be turned in a different direction.

It should not be unrealistic for nations and communities to live and function without making self-interest into a primary strategy and instead seeking the benefit of all.

If, on the other hand, nations exclusively pursue their own national self-interest, resorting primarily to force, subterfuge, and information dominance, then we will continue to create a world like the one we have. We will continue to be dominated by a hidden elite, those who have mastered the strategies of control and power.

The activist who becomes enraged by the abuse of the truth they see and who self-righteously adopts an aggressive, oppositional stance in the argument will inevitably create an opposite reaction. Blinded by self-righteousness, which is a merely self-satisfying aspect of ego, they fail to see that they are driving away exactly the unity they intend to achieve. It must be remembered that our struggle is not against people but against those forces that facilitate the control system that continually divides and oppresses humanity.

"Them and us" is a dangerous concept. There's only us. We are one human family. We are all the "children of Adam (and Eve)." Or as the poet and musician Baraka Blue wrote in a recent social media post, "All I'm really saying is that this 'us' vs. 'them' has got us in the situation we are in. We have to see everyone as 'us.' And we have to start with 'us.' If we blame 'them' we have already lost. We will never be safe until everyone in this global village is our family. Until everyone is 'us.' France is us and Palestine is us and Ferguson is us and Mali is us. I believe in us, and I love us, but I weep for us for what we do to us in the name of us."

The control system has increasingly maintained its power through the omnipresent great Lie: mind control in its many forms, the debt-based economic system, tactics of "divide and conquer" leading to perpetual war. The primary strategy in confronting the dominant culture would be to remove its primary weapons of control. Foremost among them is the fiat monetary system that has created a monopoly of money creation. Not only has this allowed a group of insiders to profit profligately, but it is the mechanism by which perpetual war can be financed. Certain governments would not be able to spend virtually infinite amounts of money to finance the military machine if it were not for the ability to create "money" out of thin air and make future generations pay.

The laws of reality, however, will not permit an egoic system to survive indefinitely, but unfortunately its end may be painful for the innocent as well as the guilty. On the one hand, it may appear, if we take a hard, honest look at those who maintain such strategies, that they seem to be ruthless, heartless, without empathy, virtually human in form alone. On the other hand, we cannot discount the possibility that there are enough people, even among those serving a control system, who have hearts, no matter how cold they may be, and that these hearts can be awakened.

The strategic question then becomes, how do we place ourselves beyond the argument, beyond the clash of opposites? How do we become the unifying solution?

Keeping our spirits up is a spiritual practice. No matter how dark it may seem, the light is growing. Deaths by war and oppression during the twentieth century were estimated at 203,000,000.[1] Despite the horrors of the present moment, the human situation is improving. Instead of being shocked at the obliviousness of many, we can keep a sense of humor, laugh at the stupidity of evil, keep striving, and keep our spirits up.

Sufis will recall the story from the time of the Prophet Muhammad of a crude Bedouin who relieved himself in the mosque, causing a disruption among the companions who then wanted to give the Bedouin a thorough thrashing. But Muhammad ended the argument by cleaning up the mess himself, telling his companions, "We have been sent to make things easy, not difficult. Make it easy, don't make it difficult."

The question remains: How do we place ourselves beyond the argument? How do we move beyond the predator/prey syndrome? How do we bring wisdom and spiritual reconciliation into a world like ours?

Might it be possible to live in such a state that we can say, "We are the enemy of no one"? Those who appear to be our enemies are actually enemies of themselves, for they are creating their own suffering, imprisoned in their own illusions and negativity.

The Divine Way should be a way of mutual support, human solidarity, sharing, and true happiness. If enough people can step into this reality, it may become clear that this happiness and virtue is a better strategy than seeking self-interest and power over others. But above all, it will become clear that spiritual laws exist and those who violate them will face consequences. Spiritual laws have a power of their own, greater than the powers of manipulation, exploitation, and domination.

In a world where so many billions of humans lack the basic conditions for a healthy and honorable life, what justification is there for the pursuit of more and more wealth only for ourselves and *our* families?

The systems and structures of competition, exclusion, privilege, and domination only compound the world's miseries. Eventually more and more of those who have been invested in the false reality will simply see the suffering they are creating for themselves and others, and simply walk away from it all.

Whether you identify with Buddha, Jesus, or Muhammad, you have an exemplar that did not make material accumulation a priority. The way of voluntary simplicity is the best road to health, happiness, justice, and humanity's survival.

22

The Axis of Being

E ACH OF US IS LIKE AN AXIS; we have this vertical dimension
within ourselves. At one end of this axis, or pole, is our individuality, our personal existence, which is largely identified with the
body. This axis runs through many levels of reality, each of increasing
subtlety: the physical, the mental, the emotional, the imaginal, the
spiritual, and even finer realms of existence, the realms of Divine Attributes, and finally all the way to the Infinite Source of Being. This
whole axis comprises the true extent of the human being. At one end
is a self and at the other end is Infinite Spirit. The infinite dimension
brings its qualities into expression in this world through that vertical
axis until it reaches its expression through our individuality.

The process of spiritual development, as we have been saying, is
a process of aligning our individuality (self, *nafs*) with Spirit, the subtlest state of our being. And *Spirit* might be explained as the "subtlest
state of everything." This individuality is the point of the cosmic Pen,
writing by the hand of God the words of the higher-order reality.

Perhaps what the friends of God have always known has something to do with what science is discovering about the zero-point field,
a dimension of virtually infinite energy, nonlocality, quantum entanglement. In this dimension, intentional thought produces immediate
effects, time and space are relativized, and the Eternal reigns.

The Sufis sometimes refer to the concept of *fana*, annihilation of
the self. Sometimes we can get confused about this. There are a lot
of distortions of this beautiful truth of fana. One distortion would

be the obliteration of individual qualities into a quality-less, uniform selflessness. You can find that in some cults. You can find that in some pathological manifestations of religious or political ideologies, where human beings become something like templates or cookie-cutter reproductions of some notion or "ideal." This is an artificial and misguided denial of our individuality, our spiritual inheritance. It's an imposition of a false concept of fana, not the real fana. You might see them wearing the uniforms of their cult or various other outward identifying traits. They have sacrificed their individualities only to unconsciously adopt a collective ego they do not recognize.

It's interesting that the Qur'an doesn't talk about fana. The only time fana is mentioned is when it says—"and upon it," this earth, everything upon it is fani, everything is passing away "except the Face of your Lord (*Rabb*)" (Qur'an, Qasas 28:88).

Everything else is passing away. So fana of the self is not something that is stressed in the Qur'an. But the subsistence of the Divine, beyond all the manifestations of time and space, is affirmed.

True Fana, the Sacred Emptiness

So what is the nature of this fana? Could this fana really mean the erasing of all individual attributes? Why, then, did Divine Intelligence create so many distinct individuals? Is this a purposeless creation?

In one sense, individuality looks like the supreme manifestation of Divine Creativity because there are so many unique beings. We should consider the true friends of God and the prophets. Did they all become personality-less? Did they lose their individuality? Or was there an individuality that was an expression of something quite mysterious, creative, and beautiful?

So fana is more something like a spacious emptiness that opens up from within your individuality. All of your best knowledge, qualities, attributes, and skills—everything that you've lived to create—is not lost, but something opens up from inside. There's an emptiness in the middle, and, importantly, there's no self-assertion there.

There's no "I" claiming anything. But those attributes and character qualities and idiosyncrasies are there for a reason. This is the creativity of the Creator. Rumi says, when describing this inner emptiness,

> Water in the boat is the ruin of the boat,
> but water under the boat is its support.
> Since Solomon cast the desire for wealth from his heart,
> he didn't call himself by any name but "poor one."
> This dervish, though in rough water,
> floats because of his or her empty heart.
> When the breath of poverty is in anyone,
> they float in peace on the waters of this life.

Mathnawi I, 985–88

The breath of poverty is a state of nonassertion, of not claiming anything for yourself. And with all that, the mature human being continues through life, accepting its sorrows and joys, while all the happiness, grief, disappointments in life, humiliation in life are not wasted or meaningless.

Individuality is something quite miraculous. Sometimes it's the poison, and sometimes it's the remedy. Sometimes it's a tyrant, and sometimes a servant. When the compulsive nafs (ego) takes control and starts asserting its autonomy and disconnects from that axis of Being, then the nafs is like Pharaoh. Pharaoh takes control and says to everyone, "I am God, and you're not." But when the Mysterion, our intrinsic being, is the active force, then the truth of the often recited phrase "There is no power nor strength except with God" is experienced. Then the self is in alignment.

So what are the examples of misalignment? Greed. Cruelty. Hypocrisy. The need to control others. Resentment. Complaining. How can a person of faith complain? What is there to complain about if you trust that the Divine Intelligence has given you *this* moment and *these* circumstances especially for the education of your soul, and every self is going through this personalized education?

There are two diametrically opposed ways to be a self in this world. One way leads to bitterness, complaining, resentment, separation, and isolation. Some people grow old with all of this written upon their faces.

The other way is when the Eternal Scales do the weighing of our lives. Our wealth, our status, our job, our name, our fame—these will not weigh for anything. What will weigh more heavily in that balance is our patience in adversity, our gratitude for everything, and our love. This is what is going to prove to be the evidence of that alignment between the self and Spirit. This will be the beauty that shines through whatever suffering has also been written upon our faces.

We read every day in the Mevlevi Wird[1] of this alignment between the self and God. These words express it beautifully:

Bismillah ar-Rahman ar-Rahim
I have readied the following words:
facing all fears, "There is no god but Allah." (*La illaha il Allah*);
facing all sorrows and sadness, "May it be as Allah wills."
    (*Ma shaa'allah*);
facing all benefits, "Praise be to Allah." (*Alhamdulillah*) And
    facing all abundance, "Thanks be to Allah." (*Shukrullah*);
facing all astonishment, "Allah is subtle beyond all knowing."
    (*Subhanallah*);
facing all sin and error, "I ask Allah's forgiveness."
    (*Astaghfirullah*);
facing all scarcities, "Allah is enough for me." (*Hasbiyallah*);
facing all calamities, "We belong to Allah and to Allah we shall
    return." (*Inna lillahi wa innaa ilayhi rajiuun*);
facing every event of destiny, "I trust in Allah." (*Tawakkaltu
    alallah*);
facing all obedience and disobedience, "There is no means or
    power in anyone except through Allah who is the Most
    High, the Most Great." (*La hawla wa la quwwata illa billahil
    alyyil azeem*)

Most Muslims would be familiar with the Arabic phrases above, but the way they are contextualized with phrases like "Facing all fears, sorrows, benefits," and so on, reveals their relationship to the vagaries of life. This could be the template for a wise life, a life given meaning through a higher order of reality.

Draw Near, a Vibrational Shift

Though Rumi's message is timeless, it is especially applicable to the particular challenges we face in this current era. It is a time when the sacred has been forgotten and replaced by material attractions. It is an era of the idolization of identity. The essential self is neglected, disregarded, forgotten, while the false self is promoted, virtual personalities interact on social media, and real human encounters become rarer.

We have been exploring the journey from ego to soul and how there is an intrinsic meaning within the human being that must not be forgotten if we are to make that journey. The soul is less a "thing" than a dimension, a knowingness.

We live in an era when computational intelligence and the analysis of mere data more and more passes for human intelligence. Human experience is being compressed into shallower dimensions until it is like an inch-deep river in which we drown.

Spiritual intelligence, the intelligence of the heart, is searching for some recognition amid these busy lives of ours.

Spiritual intelligence is about knowing what kind of questions to ask. Our capacity for asking questions, however, is crippled by ignorance of the true dimensions of our humanness. Spiritual intelligence is the widening of our context of inquiry, using capacities for knowing that are very rarely taught in schools or acknowledged in public discourse.

What do we discover in this widened context? At a certain point, the seeker becomes less interested in their own personal story and more interested in the presence and activity of the Divine.

And yet all this searching and discovery happens "within our-selves," in the deep center where we are close to God.

We have been reflecting on the secret of being human. We have been considering the qualities that result from a vibrational shift. As we become more conscious and connected with the intrinsic mean-ing within us, the Garden is brought near to the soul.

Surah Qaf, revealed approximately in the fourth year of Muham-mad's mission, describes the "Garden" offered in the afterlife and in this life for those who have "sought nearness"—that is, cultivated a conscious relationship with the Compassionate One.

> The Garden is brought near for the God-conscious.
> This is what you are promised for everyone who turns
>   (to the Real)
> and preserves (the Mysterion), who is in awe of the
>   Compassionate One in the unseen and comes with a heart
>   constantly seeking nearness. (*Surah Qaf* 50:31)

So draw near. Have that heart that is seeking nearness not only in the middle of the night, not only at the beginning of the day and at the end of the day, but at work, in moments of rest, and in our rela-tionships, so that in every relationship, in every transaction, we are living from that stillness within ourselves; we're not coming out of the anxieties of the superficial level of our being, but we're coming from the depths.

We sometimes sense there is work to do in exactly the place where we are; that the atmosphere needs some refinement, a vibra-tional shift. That is the work the friends are here to do through cere-monies like Sema, or the ritual prayers, or communal and individual zikr. This is the work of anyone who sincerely seeks to manifest the sacred. It is for us to create the kind of space where when somebody walks into that space, they come into balance, into peace.

Enter it in peace, this is the time of abiding,
in it is what they will, and We have more!
How many a generation before them
who were more powerful than they have We caused to perish.

Surah Qaf 50:36

And so, a reminder of what is at stake: whether we know it or not, we are subject to spiritual laws; a society will not change until enough people change themselves. And people will not change until they change their own inner being.

Human beings are given free will, and according to how we use this free will, we either move toward true freedom and well-being or toward the opposite, the prison of egoism.

Human beings have been given a self, and with the self is both the poison and the remedy. It is the self that can be our own worst enemy, and it is also deep within the self that the remedy of the Mysterion is found.

Seek then throughout the land, is there any refuge?

Surah Qaf 50:36

At this time in our world, we know this better than ever. The remedy we need is not to be found outside ourselves. Where are we going to flee? Are we going to leave this planet? Outwardly in this world there may be no refuge, but inwardly there is the remembrance of the awakened heart. Always.

In this, behold, there is indeed the remembrance for everyone whose heart is wide awake—that is, everyone who lends ear with a conscious mind.

Surah Qaf 50:37

The Place of Rising, a Meditation Inspired by Rumi

The work worthy of our love is the work of clearing the heart, to breathe out what needs to be released, then to move into stillness and silence. The root of every problem, every fear, and every loss of hope is the neglect of this conscious heart work.

When we live with a spiritual orientation, a *qiblah*,[2] an alignment with the Infinite, then we begin to realize a coherence of the soul formed by the magnetism of Truth. Within that coherence is peace. Crows may caw, but the fruit still ripens in the orchard. Dogs may bark, but the moon continues on its course. We are moving stage by stage, coming to understand the true dimensions of the Real.

We are eternal Spirit created by Love to know love in every condition of this life. Every circumstance of life is a step on that journey when we welcome every experience in patience and gratitude. The human essence is enriched and matured through this witnessing of experience.

The light of eternity continually shines upon this material world. As spiritual perception becomes our natural way of seeing, this earth reveals its numinous nature, just as the earth is brought to life in the springtime through friendship with spring. A thousand flowers bloom through the land when the Beloved, "Springtime," arrives.

Is the earth of our bodies any less than this worldly earth? Conscious breath, the music of glorification, the sacred dance, the inner still point—these will sanctify the body.

> Through Divine omnipotence the bodies of holy ones
> have become able to support unconditioned Light.
> God's power makes a glass vessel the dwelling place
> of that Light of which Sinai cannot bear even a speck.
> A lamp niche and a lamp glass (*Surah An-Nur* 14:35)
> have become the dwelling place of that Light
> by which Mt. Qaf[3] and Mt. Sinai[4] are broken open.
> Know that the bodies of holy ones are the lamp niche

and their hearts are the glass:
this lamp illumines the firmament.
The light of the heavens is dazzled by this Light
and vanishes like the stars in this radiance of morning.

Mathnawi VI, 3066–70

But sometimes it seems that there are only the bare branches of January, and the nightingales have hidden themselves and are mute, because the nightingale is silent without the rose garden, and only the crows are cawing as the night darkens. This is the time to remember that the Sun of Divine Knowledge has no motion and never sets. That Sun rises within the clear soul who is able to support its unconditioned light. The body can be the lamp niche in which the Sun of Divine Knowledge rises. Find the Spirit's rising place. After that, wherever you go, you will have that radiance. Any place you go will become the place of Sunrise.

Glossary

Some of the following definitions are offered for linguistic consis-
tency and clarity; some of these also carry a teaching. For example,
the definition of a dervish here is "one who stands at the threshold
between slavery and freedom." As said by Hasan Tahsin Baba, "A
definition has to cover all kindred aspects of what is being defined
and should be free from all aspects that don't agree with it."

Abundant life: Living life fully and being consciously aware of becoming whole with your mind, body, soul, and ecology.

Adab: Spiritual courtesy. This refined and conscious form of spiritual
courtesy helps to create an atmosphere of respect and affection
that supports the process of transformation. It is one of the most
important practices of the Sufi path.

Appropriateness: The child of love and humbleness.

Ashk: A Turkish term; also Farsi *eshq*. In Sufi usage, deep spiritual
love.

Attainment: The progress in using human faculties. Something is an
attainment if it can be produced at will.

Attribute: One of the Divine Qualities and Meanings that are the real
causative factors of the manifestation of material existence.

Awareness: Any perception; not necessarily "conscious."

Baqa: The state of resurrecting through the Divine Being.

Baraka: (1) Blessing. (2) When associated with an individual, it is the
ability of putting into action the Divine Attributes of supraconscious mind; "Divine charm."

Beauty: (1) An attribute of the Divine. (2) Something that becomes our point of contact with Love.

Being: (1) God—that is true Being. (2) A timeless, spaceless attribute, satisfying in itself, that can be experienced by the soul. (3) When applied to an individual, it is the degree of our identification with Spirit.

Beloved: (1) God. (2) One's point of contact with Being; it can be a single person, and it can be sensed as an omnipresent Presence.

Chivalry (*Futuwwah*): Heroic virtue, sacrifice, and generosity. The Sufi ethic that traces back to the family of the Prophet.

Completion: In the case of an individual human, it is being one with the Whole, realizing Truth.

Complete human being (*insāni kāmil*): The fully mature human being; someone whose self has become transparent to God and thus can reflect the Divine Attributes appropriately.

Consciousness: The degree of our awareness, inner and outer, on as many levels of our experience as are available to us. A potentially comprehensive awareness that encompasses thinking, feeling, and bodily sensation without being limited by them.

Contentment: In Arabic, *qanaat*. Knowing that you have; an awareness of one's present richness without precluding having more.

Denier: In Arabic, *kafir*. One who denies the reality of a beneficent Unseen order. We reject the dogmatic notion that a kafir is a "non-Muslim."

Dergah: A Persian word for a Sufi training center. Synonyms: *tekkye* (Turkish), *zawia* (North African); *khaneqah* (Persian and Indian).

Dervish: A person who has committed themselves to the Sufi path; one who stands at the threshold between slavery and freedom.

Discernment: In Arabic, *furqan*. An innate capacity within the human being to discern the good and the true, the real from the false.

Discipline: Methodical pursuit; the state of someone who does everything for a purpose.

Ecology: Relationship with our environment.

Ego: In Arabic, *nafs*. (1) The self, which is that which we will always continue to transform and develop into ever more subtle and spiritualized states of being. (2) The lower self.

Egoism: The self in its more compulsive manifestations. The self-righteousness of the intellect working for its own survival at the expense of the whole self.

Elder: A mature carrier of the Teaching; a light-holder of the tradition.

Emancipation: Freedom from the fear of loss.

Essence: (1) For the human being: one's innate nature. (2) In general, the essential nature of anything; that which is inherently and practically good in something.

Essential self: The individual consciousness minus the conditioning of the false self; personal consciousness, experienced as the objective witness before it is socialized or conditioned.

Faith: In Arabic, *iman*. (1) The perception and understanding that existence is purposeful, intelligent, and beneficent. (2) Hope substantiated by knowledge.

Fana: The state of the self having melted into the Divine Being, which is followed by or alternates with **baqa.**

Freedom: Having will; being free of negativity; doing what one chooses without hurting anyone.

God: (1) The absolute source of all that exists. (2) The Whole. (3) The subtlest state of everything.

Grace: The continuous overflowing of the Divine that is coming to all beings, all witnesses of God. The amount of grace we receive primarily depends on our ability to receive it.

Heart: (1) The true cognitive center of our individuality or soul. (2) The subconscious and supraconscious faculties of mind, primarily nonintellectual. (3) The midpoint between self and Spirit, which allows a connection to be formed between them.

Higher Self: That part of ourselves that is in contact with the Creative Power, or Divine Being.

Himma: Spiritual resolve. A degree of spiritual intention accompanied by yearning. See also Intention.

Hu: The pronoun of Divine Presence, also understood by Sufis to be the indwelling presence of Allah.

Human being: A vehicle for individualized Spirit; the most complete witness of Spirit within this material world.

Humbleness: (1) The awareness of our dependence on Spirit, that we are not the originators of anything but the reflectors of the attributes of Spirit. (2) The awareness of our interdependence with and need for other human beings.

Imaginal: See Interworld.

Iman: See Faith.

Innate nature: In Arabic, *fitra*. The natural disposition that God has instilled in the human being.

Intellect: (1) Thought, distinguished from the faculties of the subconscious and supraconscious mind; mind activated by will and reason. The faculty of mind most under our immediate control. (2) See Universal Intellect.

Intention: In Arabic, *himma*. An aim or wish, clearly formulated in words, by which we mobilize the energy to attain that aim or wish. Having a spiritual intention (*himma*) is the beginning of integrity.

Interdependence: The recognized need of human beings for one another in order to attain the fullness of life on all levels, from material to cosmic.

Interworld: In Arabic, *barzakh*. *Mundus imaginalis*, a visionary realm intermediate between pure meaning and material existence; the locus of imaginal experience.

Knowledge: Seven levels are recognized: knowing something's name, or from merely hearing of it; knowing through the senses by direct experience; knowing about something in its manifold aspects as a result of normal experience; knowing through a deeper grasp involving the subtler aspects of perception and understanding; knowing through skillful doing; knowing through the supraconscious faculties; knowing by "Spirit plus nothing."

Kufr: Denial. The tendency in human beings to be in denial of the spiritual nature of reality. Sometimes mistranslated as misbelief or infidelity, and incorrectly applied to non-Muslims.

Leader: In the spiritual context, someone who is "lifted up" by others in order to be of service, to get a particular job done, to whom we give love, respect, and everything necessary to get the job done.

Life: An attribute of God. It is from eternity to eternity and forms our existence.

Love: The greatest transforming power; our experience of Spirit; the electromagnetic milieu in which we all exist, which exerts various forces of attraction among all that it contains. The final purpose of everything.

Lower self: The self based on ego.

Mathnawi: Rumi's six volume masterwork of more than twenty thousand couplets, containing stories, allegories, sublime supplications, jokes, and metaphysical reflections. Rumi's lyrical poems and quatrains are contained in another collection known as Kulliyeti Shams, Divani Kabir, or Divani Shams.

Maturity: Skillfulness within our particular ecology, which comes from the development and balance of latent human faculties under Divine grace and guidance. It leads to fulfillment in every department of life.

Meditation: Listening within; a function of conscious awareness, not intellect.

Mevlana (or Mawlana): "Our Master," an honorific commonly applied to Jalaluddin Rumi.

Mind: (1) The totality of our faculties for knowing. (2) The whole field of reality.

Mysterion: The inner capacity that helps the human being to discern the Real from the illusory. The innermost essence, "the intrinsic meaning" of the human.

Mysticism: A faculty peculiar to the human being, which is neither obvious to the intellect nor the senses but that depends on the refinement and receptivity of faculties within the supraconscious mind, including developing a receptivity to the Divine at the deepest levels of the subconscious.

Nafs: See Ego.

Nothingness: The point reached by utmost subtilization. Like sugar dissolving in water, the self is not really gone but transparent to the Divine Presence.

Personality: Learned habits of thought, feeling, and behavior; the social self. Personality can manifest our essence or obscure it.

Point of contact: A person, saint, or prophet through whom we gain access to Higher Self or an experience of the Divine.

Presence: (1) The state of being consciously aware of all our faculties (physical, mental, emotional, spiritual) simultaneously. (2) The infinite Divine milieu in which we exist.

Prophet: A person chosen to bring a message (from the Divine) or a code of living, a sacred way of life for the general population. A prophet may also initiate a small group of close companions into knowledge of Truth.

Rabb: "Sustainer," "Lord," "Educator"; that aspect of the Divine that educates our souls. A synonym for Allah, the Rabb al-Alameen, Lord and Sustainer of All Worlds.

Rabita: An affectionate bond formed between a dervish and shaikh, student and spiritual guide, in which spiritual support and protection are maintained beyond time and space.

Realization: Understanding reached through our mobilization of the supraconscious and subconscious minds as well as our five senses.

Remembering, Remembrance: In Arabic, zikr. (1) Conscious awareness of our relationship with the Divine. (2) Repetition of the Divine Name(s).

Revelation: A communication of the Divine for the sake of guidance; instructions for the realization of our true human nature from the Source of our human nature; the Holy Books (explicitly Torah, Psalms, Gospels, Qur'an; implicitly the sacred books of all traditions).

Sacred Law: In Arabic, *shari'ah*. A code of living based upon the Qur'an and the example (*sunnah*) of Muhammad, the intention of which is to restore and safeguard our humanness and the social order.

Secret: In Arabic, *sirr*. See Mysterion.

Self: The sense of identity, that with which we are always working. At the lowest level, it can be a complex of psychological manifestations arising from the body and related to its pleasure and survival. At its highest level, it can be experienced as an infinitely fine substance. (See also Soul; Spirit.)

Sema: In the Mevlevi tradition this is the ceremony of the whirling dervishes, involving a precise choreography, supported by a classical tradition of music, and the intention of which is worship. In other Sufi lineages, it may be a ceremonial gathering involving music and zikr.

Sensing: A spiritual practice based in being grounded in an awareness of the body.

Service: (1) Action benefiting something greater than oneself. (2) The natural outcome of being connected to cosmic energy.

Shaikh: In Sufism a shaikh is a person who has been given the spiritual authority and permission (*ijazet*) by a lineage, typically through another shaikh who has trained them, to represent the teaching of that lineage.

Shari'ah: See Sacred Law.

Sin: (1) Separation from the Divine Reality; the opposite of submission; saying no to God. (2) Personal choice that harms or degrades our humanness.

Soul: Individualized Spirit. The result of the degree of connection between self and Spirit. The core of individuality that can be developed and spiritualized. See also Self; Spirit.

Spirit: (1) The first or primary manifestation of the Absolute. (2) As an attribute of the human being, it is our innermost consciousness (Holy Spirit; *Ruh*, in Arabic). Spirit is one pole, while self is the opposite pole. According to the Qur'an, Spirit is described as an impulse or command (*amr*) from God. Spirit is the essence of life itself. It is like a nondimensional point that is linked to the realm of Unity and has access to the realm of Divine Attributes, the Divine Names. (See also Self; Soul.)

Submission: (1) A translation of *islam*, the Arabic word linguistically related to peace and wholeness. (2) Lower self bowing to Higher Self; listening to the directive of Higher Self wherever we find it.

Subtle faculties: In Arabic, *lataif*. Literally, "subtleties"; capacities of the human nervous system to reflect the one Creative Energy: for example, just as the brain is the platform of intellectual mind, which is one kind of reflection of the Creative Energy, there are other, subtler faculties that can apprehend the infinite qualities of Being.

Sufi: A person traveling on the way of love leading to Divine Truth. A word whose root means "pure" and "unadulterated."

Sufism: In Arabic, *tasawwuf*. The practice of self-purification under the auspices of Divine Love, leading to beautiful character and a profound inner life.

Supraconscious: Faculties of the human mind that are subtle and beyond the "thinking" mind; a synonym for "heart."

Truth: The knowledge that "I" am not separate from the Whole. In relation to the manifest world, everything that exists is created "with the Truth" according to the Qur'an.

Universal Intellect: The Intelligence of the Whole.

Unseen: In Arabic, *al-Ghaib*. Those aspects of reality beyond our perception.

Will: The faculty of conscious choice; the ability to "do" consciously; a unique attribute of the human being.

Wisdom: Knowledge that comes from within; knowledge in harmony with spiritual laws.

Worship: Loving respect for a higher spiritual power; a yearning found in human beings.

Yearning: One of the most valuable attributes of a seeker, which becomes the motivating force of the whole journey of return to God.

Zikr: See Remembering, Remembrance.

Notes

A Note on Language and Translation

1. A "sacred saying" from Muhammad (peace be upon him) in which he relates a truth revealed by God. Sometimes these are spiritual sayings current in the culture of his time that can be attributed to earlier sources, and sometimes, as in this case, they may be strikingly original.

Chapter 2. From Ego to Soul

1. The line of poetry is quoted by Rumi, with slight variance, from the *Diwan* of al-Mutanabbi, p. 93.
2. *Signs of the Unseen*, Translated by Wheeler Thackston (Putney, Vermont: Threshold Books, 1994).
3. The "pronoun" of Divine Presence.

Chapter 5. Human Weakness, Cosmic Mercy

1. The "knowers," not necessarily the gnostics of the early Christian period.
2. John Renard, trans., *Ibn Abbad of Ronda* (Mahwah, NJ: Paulist Press, 1986), 70.
3. From the hadith collections Muslim, Nasai, and Tirmidhi.
4. Renard, *Ibn Abbad of Ronda*, 154.
5. The Sufi term for that disordered complex of ego drives that govern our lives when we are not in resonance with Spirit.

Chapter 6. Attention and Our Inner Being

1. A Sufi term for the spiritual seeker who has voluntarily taken on the "work of the soul."

CHAPTER 7. THE WORK OF THE SOUL

1. *Rumi's Sun: The Teachings of Shams of Tabriz*, trans. Refik Algan and Camille Adams Helminski (Louisville, KY: Threshold Books, 2017), 177.
2. https://theteachingsofrobertrhondellgibson.blogspot.com.

CHAPTER 9. CONDITIONS FOR THE SUFI PROCESS

1. *Baraka* literally means "blessing." Its specialized meaning here is the effective grace transmitted from a lineage of masters, saints, and prophets.
2. The whirling ceremony of the Mevlevi tradition. It can also refer to zikr ceremonies involving music, usually flute, percussion, and voice.
3. From Abdulbaki Golpinarli, *Mevlevilik sonra Mevlanadan*, trans. Nilufer Devecigil and Kabir Helminski.
4. From Abdulbaki Golpinarli, *Mevlevilik sonra Mevlanadan*, trans. Nilufer Devecigil and Kabir Helminski.
5. *Kash al-Muhjub*, trans. Reynold A. Nicholson (London: Gibb Memorial Trust, 2014), an early Persian treatise on Sufism by Ali al-Hujwiri.
6. Here he is referring to a dogmatic, legalistic way of life, without the benefit of *ashq*, Divine Love, which the Sufis, the people of tariqah, consider essential to Islam itself.
7. Abdulbaki Golpinarli, *Mevlevilik sonra Mevlanadan*, trans. Nilufer Devecigil and Kabir Helminski.

CHAPTER 11. THE QUEEN OF INTELLIGENCES

1. From *The Pocket Rumi*, ed. Kabir Helminski (Boulder: Shambhala Publications, 2017), 3.
2. Sufi training center.
3. Unpublished translation by Refik Algan and Kabir Helminski.

CHAPTER 12. SPIRITUAL PERCEPTION

1. Kabir Helminski, *The Knowing Heart: The Sufi Path of Transformation* (Boston: Shambhala Publications, 1999), 191.
2. The night of Muhammad's spiritual ascension through the levels of reality, the "heavens," when he was brought near to Allah.
3. From *Rumi's Sun: The Teachings of Shams of Tabriz*, trans. Refik Algan and Camille Adams Helminski (Louisville, KY: Threshold Books, 2017).

CHAPTER 13. SHOW US THINGS AS THEY ARE

1. In the hadith collections of Bukhari and Muslim.
2. In the hadith collections of Bukhari and Muslim.

CHAPTER 15. THE FOUNDATIONS OF HEARTFULNESS

1. Kabir Helminski, *Living Presence: A Sufi Way to Mindfulness and the Essential Self* (New York: Putnam, 1992).
2. The "We" here refers to the Divine in Its totality, our "Sustainer" (*Rabb*).
3. From *Love's Ripening*, trans. Kabir Helminski and Ahmad Rezwani (Boston: Shambhala Publications, 2008), 144.

CHAPTER 16. LIGHT UPON LIGHT: A PARABLE

1. Horse lovers may also know that horses in a certain settings can contribute to the healing of human beings, especially autistic or traumatized individuals. Our daughter has worked in equine therapy and has shared with us some amazing examples of horses demonstrating a high level of awareness, mirroring, even "teaching," human beings. So we should also allow that the "horse," which is our body, may also teach the rider, though this does not negate the point that Rumi is making here. Presence leads to a reciprocal awareness that benefits both horse and rider.

CHAPTER 17. PERSONAL SOVEREIGNTY

1. *The Pocket Rumi*, ed. Kabir Helminski. (Boulder: Shambhala Publications, 2017)
2. *The Pocket Rumi*, ed. Kabir Helminski. (Boulder: Shambhala Publications 2017)
3. The Símurgh, a mythical bird capable of flying into the Divine Presence.
4. A hadith. "Presence" is the concentration of the mind on God. See Kabir Edmund Helminski, *Living Presence: A Sufi Way to Mindfulness and the Essential Self* (New York: Jeremy P. Tarcher /Putnam, 1992).

CHAPTER 18. COHERENCE OF THE SOUL

1. An invisible, subtle field of coherence that exists due to the nonlocal quantum entanglement of elements within the field.
2. A more thorough discussion of this subject is found in "Grapes Ripen Smiling at One Another," in my book *The Knowing Heart: A Sufi Path of Transformation* (Boston: Shambhala Publications, 1999).
3. *Mathnawi* IV, beginning line 40.
4. Rumi, Ghazal, unpublished translation by Kabir Helminski and Leila Bahreinian. https://ganjoor.net/moulavi/shams/ghazalsh/sh322.
5. Suleyman Hayati Loras, d. 1985 in Konya, Turkey.
6. Bruce Miller, *Rumi Comes to America: How the Poet of Mystical Love Arrived on our Shores* (Decatur, GA: Miller Media, 2017).

CHAPTER 19. HIGHER-ORDER REALITY

1. From an esoteric perspective, the Islamic term *shaytan* represents forces of dispersion, denial, "evil" within the ego.

CHAPTER 20. LIFE IN THE WORLD

1. From Isabel Burton, *The Inner Life of Syria, Palestine, and the Holy Land*, 1875, vol. II, cited in Mary S. Lovell, *A Rage to Live: A Biography of Richard and Isabel Burton* (New York: W. W. Norton & Company 2000), 513.
2. *Le Siècle* newspaper, August 2, 1869.
3. Michel Chodkiewicz, *The Spiritual Writings of Amir `Abd al-Kader al-Jazari* (New York: SUNY Press, 1995), 205.
4. Michel Chodkiewicz, *The Spiritual Writings of Amir `Abd al-Kader al-Jazari* (New York: SUNY Press, 1995), 176.
5. *Surah al-Anfal*, 8:17: "Thou didst not throw when thou threwest, but Allah threw." When the Prophet Muhammad picked up handful of gravel and threw it, the whole battle turned in their favor. This verse is beloved to mystics who read in it the state of fana, selfless action.

CHAPTER 21. ONENESS ON THE WORLD STAGE

1. "Estimated Metrics for the Entire 20th Century" in *Necrometrics*, http://necrometrics.com/all20c.htm.

CHAPTER 22. THE AXIS OF BEING

1. A book that is a litany of prayers and Qur'anic selections read daily by people on the Mevlevi path, the followers of the way of Rumi.
2. Conventionally, the direction of prayer of which a Muslim is cognizant, i.e., toward the Kaaba in Mecca.
3. The mythical mountains that surround the ends of the earth.
4. The mountain on which Moses received the revelation of the Torah.

Bibliography

Books on Sufism

Helminski, Kabir. *Holistic Islam: Sufism, Transformation, and the Needs of Our Time.* Louisville, KY: Threshold Books, 2019.

———. *In the House of Remembering: The Living Tradition of Sufi Teaching.* Louisville, KY: Threshold Books, 2020.

———. *The Knowing Heart: A Sufi Path of Transformation.* Boston: Shambhala Publications, 2000.

———. *Living Presence: The Sufi Path to Mindfulness and the Essential Self.* 25th anniversary ed. New York: TarcherPerigee, 2017.

Translations of Rumi

Helminski, Camille, and Kabir Helminski, trans. *Jewels of Remembrance: A Daybook of Spiritual Guidance Containing 365 Selections from the Wisdom of Rumi.* Boston: Shambhala Publications, 2000.

———. *Rumi: Daylight—a Daybook of Spiritual Guidance.* Boston: Shambhala Publications, 2000.

Helminski, Kabir, trans. *Love Is a Stranger: Selected Lyric Poetry of Jalaluddin Rumi.* Boston: Threshold Books and Shambhala Publications, 1992.

———. *The Pocket Rumi.* Boulder: Shambhala Publications, 2017.

———. *Ruins of the Heart: Selected Lyric Poetry of Jelaluddin Rumi.* Putney, VT: Threshold Books, 1980.

Helminski, Kabir, and Ahmad Rezwani, trans. *Love's Ripening: Rumi on the Heart's Journey.* Boston: Shambhala Publications, 2010.

Helminski, Kabir, and Camille Helminski, trans. *The Rumi Daybook: 365 Poems and Teachings from the Beloved Sufi Master.* Boston: Shambhala Publications, 2012.

Thackston, Wheeler, trans. *Signs of the Unseen, Discourses of Rumi.* Putney, VT: Threshold Books, 1994

RELATED TITLES

Algan, Refik, and Camille Adams Helminski, trans. *Rumi's Sun: The Teachings of Shams of Tabriz* Louisville, KY: Threshold Books, 2017.

Helminski, Camille Adams. *Women of Sufism: A Hidden Treasure.* Boston: Shambhala Publications, 2003.

———. *Rumi and His Friends: Stories of the Lovers of God.* Louisville, KY: Fons Vitae, 2013.

Helminski, Camille, and Mahmoud Mostafa, trans. *The Mevlevi Wird: The Prayers Recited Daily by Mevlevi Dervishes.* Putney, VT: Threshold Books, 1989.

Helminski, Kabir, trans. *Civilization of Paradise: Asad Ali.* Louisville, KY: Fons Vitae, 2014.

Helminski, Kabir, and Refik Algan, trans. *The Drop That Became the Sea, Lyric Poems of Yunus Emre.* Boston: Shambhala Publications, 1989.

Helminski, Kabir, Camille Helminski, and Ibrahim Shihabi, trans. *Happiness without Death: Asad Ali*, Louisville, KY: Threshold Books, 1994.

ISLAMIC SUBJECTS

Asad, Muhammad, trans. *The Message of the Quran.* Los Angeles: Book Foundation, 2008.

Eaton, Charles le Gai. *The Book of Hadith, Sayings of the Prophet Mohammed.* Edited by Kabir Helminski. Los Angeles: Book Foundation, 2008.

Helminski, Camille, ed. *The Book of Character: Writings on Character and Virtue from Islamic and Other Sources.* Los Angeles: Book Foundation, 2005.

———. *The Book of Nature: A Sourcebook of Spiritual Perspectives on Nature and the Environment.* Los Angeles: Book Foundation, 2006.

Helminski, Kabir. *The Book of Language: A Deep Glossary of Islamic and English Spiritual Terms.* Los Angeles: Book Foundation, 2006.

———. *The Book of Revelations: A Sourcebook of Selections from the Quran with Interpretations.* Los Angeles: Book Foundation, 2005.